T0323511

The Stoic Educator

Stoic wisdom has become popular for helping us focus on what we can and can't control in life. But how can Stoic philosophies help you in your specific role as a teacher?

Emir Cruz Fernández has the answers in this useful new book. Drawing on the insights of Marcus Aurelius, Epictetus, Seneca, and other great philosophers, he shows how Stoic wisdom and the four Stoic virtues can help you improve classroom management, handle difficult or toxic colleagues, overcome imposter syndrome, master your sphere of influence, control reactions, thrive in the face of adversity, develop resilience, and more.

Many of the challenges in the education world feel overwhelming and out of our control, but with Stoic philosophies, we can take control of the narrative and free ourselves from the things we cannot change—only focusing on the ones we can. With wisdom, courage, and perseverance, join Emir on the journey to finding a more fulfilling path in your career.

EMIR CRUZ FERNÁNDEZ is a philologist, actor, and committed educator. He is the author of the award-winning book *Muslims of Spain, Marvel Education*, and the forthcoming *The Odyssey of Teaching*.

The Stoic Educator

STRATEGIES FOR TEACHER
WELL-BEING AND MASTERING
CHALLENGES WITH GRACE

Emir Cruz Fernández

Routledge
Taylor & Francis Group

NEW YORK AND LONDON

Designed cover image: Getty Images

First published 2025
by Routledge
605 Third Avenue, New York, NY 10158

and by Routledge
4 Park Square, Milton Park, Abingdon, Oxon, OX14 4RN

Routledge is an imprint of the Taylor & Francis Group, an informa business

© 2025 Emir Cruz Fernández

ISBN: 978-1-032-87971-0 (hbk)
ISBN: 978-1-032-84138-0 (pbk)
ISBN: 978-1-003-53565-2 (ebk)

DOI: 10.4324/9781003535652

Typeset in Minion
by SPi Technologies Private Limited, India (STRAIVE)

Dedicated to the Stoic educators who, day by day, work hard to make this a better world. And to the first three Stoic philosophers I met:

José Cruz, my grandfather

R. Leonardo Cruz, my father

José A. Cruz, my uncle

Whose wisdom, resilience, and commitment to virtue have been a guiding light on my journey.

Contents

Contents

Contents

Meet the Author

 **Emir Cruz Fernández** has studied Psychology, Theater, Literature, Art, and languages at Lehman College, the CUNY Graduate Center, the Universidad de Alcalá de Henares in Spain, and CALES (Center for Arabic Language and Eastern Studies) in Sana'a, Yemen. He holds a PhD in Spanish Golden Age Literature from the CUNY Graduate Center. Dr. Cruz Fernández is a philologist, actor, and committed educator. He is also the author of the award-winning book *Muslims of Spain, Marvel Education*, and the forthcoming *The Odyssey of Teaching*. His passion for learning is a testament to his commitment to education and the arts.

Introduction

DOI: 10.4324/9781003535652-1

****

It does not matter what period of the year you are in: if you have bought this book, you are likely struggling. If it is the beginning of the term, you are trying to find a way to have your students listen to you and earn their respect. If the middle, then you are likely trying to navigate difficulties that come up during the year and the daily challenges we face while trying to teach, moderate, and educate teenagers. Finally, if you are at the end of the term, well, there is no other way to say this: you are exhausted and most likely looking forward to your next vacation.

Let me tell you, I can relate. The challenges are many, and we tend to feel overwhelmed by them—especially when we feel there is no way out. Sometimes, we are under the impression that we have tried anything and everything but nothing seems to work. There is no getting through to these young minds and making them see the importance of what they are living. Of what they are learning. On the impact the present will have on their future.

And that is where I come in. If you're reading this book, you should know that I have been teaching for over 20 years in public high schools and universities, dealing with the most diverse and challenging situations. I want you to understand that I have walked the same path as you, facing similar hurdles and triumphs. I am here to offer you tools to help you navigate these challenges. I understand your pain because I have experienced it, too. I also know that these difficulties are causing a shortage of teachers, with fewer people wanting to work in the educational system every term.

The problems are many: lack of support, financial impediments for investments, lack of discipline from the students, and an old administrative structure which the schools need to adhere to. Students are learning less, and teachers are getting sicker and more burned out with the stress they must deal with, all without support. *But how will we help the younger generations? How do we take control of the narrative?*

How do we prepare ourselves to deal with the challenges we must face every single day? I know how you feel. But it is up to us to change if nothing else does.

As you will see in this book, one of the Stoic principles is to free yourself from the things you cannot control—instead, you must deal with the ones you can. And once you learn this, you will feel less stressed and know that if you can control it, *you can change it.* And if you can change it, you can make it better.

Stoicism as a tool for teaching and self-improvement

In the beginning of my career, it was hard to understand that what I had learned in school was not what I was going to apply in the classroom. Or maybe that I was not taught in the university what I needed to do to navigate the public school system. I had no experience in being a teacher, did not know how to deal with troublesome students, and did not know how to navigate tricky situations with administration and colleagues. I felt lost. And I am not going to lie; sometimes, I just felt like I wanted to give up.

But this would not be me, and, thus, I decided not to quit but rather to persevere. I discovered, as time went by, that experience is the greatest teacher. I used trial and error. I studied. I learned to focus on the things that I can change and control. I was all about changing my mindset.

And how does an old philosophical school such as Stoicism fit it? How can it help me? As you will see in this book, it is all about changing the way we see things. It is about our perceptions, thoughts, and the actions that we take. I learned that it *was* possible to get rid of the toxic environment and focus on the positive. That we can change things if we focus on what we can control. Granted, it wasn't easy. But I can assure you that if I could make it, you can as well.

But I must warn you: This process is as challenging as it is transformational. It is not easy to change the preconceptions we have about people, situations, and learning to be resilient or turn the other cheek. It is hard to let go of the things we previously believed in and make a 180-degree turn and change our minds completely. It requires dedication, persistence, and a bit of courage. It will also require the wisdom to reflect on oneself and see what it is that you need to change. It is about applying justice to the processes as you experience them.

I invite you to join me in this journey toward finding a fulfilling path that will certainly change your life, as it changed mine. In a short time, you will see it modify your relationship with students, administration, parents, and all of those who are involved in the school environment. As usual, I will use my real-life stories (although the names have been changed) to show you examples of how to apply this to your life. Are you ready to see your life in the educational system change for the better?

CHAPTER 1

Stoic Wisdom Unleashed

Ancient Insights for Modern Educators

DOI: 10.4324/9781003535652-2

> " You have power over your mind—not outside events. Realize this, and you will find strength.

Marcus Aurelius, *Meditations*

If you sometimes feel that you have tried everything and nothing has worked, I want to propose that you try something different. I would like you to consider incorporating the Stoic philosophy into your life. This ancient way of thinking is based on two mindsets that will certainly resonate with you. The first is that we are responsible for how we view things and that this is the true cause of suffering. The second is to learn to accept the things we cannot control.

Think about it this way: if you have an outing planned with your class and it starts raining, there is not much you can do. You don't control the weather. However, you *can* control giving them an alternative that will not involve them getting wet. There is no use in mourning the fact that it is raining. There is nothing you can do to change that. Therefore, the faster you accept that this is something you cannot control, the less you will suffer.

In this chapter, we will explore the profound world of Stoic philosophy. We will delve into its principles, values, and beliefs. I will share my journey of discovering this ancient wisdom. This exploration forms the foundation for the rest of the book, where we will witness how embracing a Stoic approach can transform us into more effective educators—true Stoic educators. Rest assured, the efficacy of this approach is unquestionable. The Stoic philosophy's profound impact on our lives is evident through its influence on modern practices, like cognitive behavioral therapy (CBT).

The origins of Stoicism

The Stoic philosophy originated in ancient Greece and gained significant popularity during the Roman era. Although some scholars debate the direct influence of the great Greek philosophers Socrates, Plato, and Aristotle on the development of Stoicism, it is widely acknowledged that Stoic philosophy emerged after their time. The Greek philosopher Zeno of Citium is credited with developing Stoicism around the 3rd century BCE. His line of thought was influenced by the three previously mentioned philosophers (Mind of a Stoic, n.d.).

All of these discoveries occurred during the Hellenistic Age (from the death of Alexander the Great in 323 BCE to the Roman conquest of Egypt in 30 BCE). This transitional period marked a time of significant change following the decline of the Greek empire. While Athens remained an intellectual hub, the political chaos of the era brought about various transformations. In this environment, within the influential city of Athens, Stoicism emerged and flourished, gaining widespread acceptance among the prominent thinkers of the time.

In this context, it is important to understand that the Stoic school of thought is typically divided into three distinct periods, each characterized by a different period in time and the evolution of the philosophy. These periods are commonly known as the Early Stoa (3rd century BCE), Middle Stoa (2nd and 1st centuries BCE), and Late Stoa (1st and 2nd centuries CE). Owing to the scarcity of surviving documents from the Early and Middle Stoic periods, scholars often rely on works of the Late Stoa for the most ancient sources of Stoic thought.

The "Early Stoa" denotes the initial period of Stoicism, representing its foundational stage. During this period, notable thinkers such as Zeno articulated the philosophy by dividing it into three fundamental components: logic, physics, and ethics. Zeno established the framework by regarding logic as a tool, considering physical theory as the means to determine correct action, and recognizing ethics as the bedrock of knowledge. He viewed the wise person as embodying human excellence (Saunders, 2023). Zeno's formative ideas for Stoicism drew significant influence from his studies of Socratic and Platonic philosophies.

One notable aspect of the Early Stoa is the incorporation of *logos*, the Greek term for logic, in Zeno's early writings. He emphasized the importance of exercising reason and deliberation rather than succumbing to impulsive behaviors and passions. According to his teachings, individuals should engage their logical faculties to assess situations and make informed choices. The philosopher believed that applying logic to life represented a deliberate and measured approach, starkly contrasting to impulsivity and passion. Zeno regarded this capacity for reasoned thinking as a defining characteristic distinguishing humans from animals, offering the potential for a more meaningful and fulfilling existence (The Collector, 2022a).

Stoicism gained significant popularity during the Late Stoa when Rome had established itself as an empire and expanded its dominion over various territories. The abundance of preserved documents from this time allows us to gain extensive knowledge about Stoicism, including its most prominent figures such as Seneca, Epictetus, and the Roman emperor Marcus Aurelius. While we cannot discount the potential contributions of those from the Middle Stoa, the need for historical documentation limits our ability to provide precise details. Nevertheless, it is evident that during this period, the school of thought evolved and adapted while upholding the fundamental principles of logic, wisdom, practicality, and reason, which remained the enduring cornerstones of Stoicism (The Collector, 2022a).

Returning to the Late Stoa, we find that the emperor Marcus Aurelius's profound embrace of Stoicism not only played a crucial role in disseminating its teachings but also left an indelible mark on history. His deep affinity for philosophy's principles of law, justice, morality, natural science, nature, and providence (Saunders, 2023) was a testament to the enduring power of Stoicism. Despite subsequent emperors sharing different levels of enthusiasm for understanding and adopting Stoicism, its influence in spreading concepts like Christianity and Roman law as the empire expanded cannot be understated. However, over time, Stoicism gradually faded into the background.

Stoicism, with its enduring relevance, resurfaced in the Renaissance and the Age of Enlightenment, shaping the course of history. In the present day, Stoicism is experiencing a significant resurgence, a testament to its timeless wisdom and practicality. This resurgence is partly due to contemporary authors and public figures who are not only highlighting its practical applications for modern life but also demonstrating its enduring value in navigating today's challenges. Works by authors like Ryan Holiday have brought Stoic principles into the mainstream, further solidifying its place in our contemporary world.

The four Stoic virtues

In the realm of Stoicism, understanding philosophy goes hand in hand with embracing the power of its four cardinal virtues. These virtues form the bedrock of Stoic wisdom and serve as guiding principles for moral and ethical living. Like the guiding stars, these virtues illuminate our path, aiding us in decision-making. As we contemplate each virtue, pondering its application to our present circumstances, we unlock the answers to life's intricate question: "What should I do?" Regardless of the domain of our existence, these virtues provide an unwavering compass, pointing us toward the path of fulfillment and purpose. Welcome to a transformative journey where the timeless teachings of Stoicism converge with your unique voyage of self-discovery.

Within Stoicism, these virtues are cherished as essential qualities that individuals should cultivate and carry on their lifelong journey. They are the guiding stars, illuminating the path, leading us to take the right course of action, regardless of the tumultuous winds surrounding us. Now, what are these four virtues that hold such profound significance? Allow me to unveil their transformative power.

They are wisdom, courage, temperance, and justice. Although these virtues may sound familiar, their Stoic interpretation and application offer a unique perspective, setting them apart from our conventional understanding. Their importance and the perception we have of them have changed throughout time as our values modify. As we delve deeper into their essence, we shall unravel the subtle nuances and unveil their tremendous potential to shape our lives. So let us embark on this transformative odyssey, where Stoic wisdom intertwines with your journey of self-discovery.

Wisdom

Wisdom, or *sophia*, the cornerstone of Stoicism, holds immense significance on the path to personal growth and understanding. This beacon guides us to discern between right and wrong, continuously seeking enlightenment. Within the Stoic framework, wisdom encompasses more than just knowledge; it is the profound understanding of what is good, bad, and indifferent. Through wisdom, we can discern what aids our flourishing and fulfillment in life and what hinders our progress (Robertson, 2019). Embracing wisdom empowers us to perceive life's truths, illuminating the boundaries of our control. With this clarity, we can confidently navigate any situation that presents itself. Wisdom grants us the knowledge to shape our actions, ensuring that they align with our pursuit of happiness and harmony.

As we embrace wisdom, we gain a remarkable ability to distinguish the essence of what truly matters in life. When we hone our discernment, decision-making becomes infused with clarity and purpose. In a world inundated with endless information, the wisdom we seek becomes a guiding force that filters through the noise. It empowers us to separate profound insights that lead to a good life from the mere accumulation of data (Holiday, 2019). Through the lens of wisdom, we gain the precious gift of perspective, enabling us to make choices that align with our values and aspirations.

Let us embark on this transformative journey of wisdom, where the pursuit of truth and self-mastery awaits. By cultivating wisdom, we transcend the superficial and access the profound understanding that leads to a life well lived. Discover the boundless wisdom that awaits you, unravel the intricacies of life, and embark on a path of clarity, purpose, and fulfillment. Through the power of wisdom, we unlock the keys to living a truly extraordinary life.

Courage

Let us now explore the remarkable virtue of courage, or *andreia*, which takes us on a journey beyond the mere conquest of fear. When envisioning courage, we often picture ourselves scaling towering mountains, walking across dizzying bridges, or diving fearlessly into shark-infested waters. These scenarios align with our conventional understanding of courage. However, according to the Stoics, courage extends far beyond confronting fear. It encompasses our resolute determination to act, even in discomfort and trepidation. This virtue guides us through the labyrinth of challenges, adversities, and uncertainties that life presents.

While the Stoics acknowledge fear as a natural human emotion, they emphasize the significance of meeting adversity head-on, with unwavering willingness. It is about taking purposeful action and summoning the necessary energy to overcome obstacles. In doing so, we act in harmony with the greater good, transcending personal feelings or thoughts about the situation or individuals involved. Moreover, when we contemplate courage, we must return to the core Stoic principle of discerning what lies within our sphere of control.

As we embrace courage, we must remember that our encounters with adversity should be approached with calculated intent, free from recklessness. Instead, we employ wisdom to assess situations, comprehending the potential consequences of our actions. Acting in accordance with reason and our moral compass, we demonstrate Stoic courage, which surpasses mere risk-taking, defying death, or weathering misfortune. It is the courage to stand for our fellow human beings' well-being and remain steadfast in our principles when others abandon theirs. It is the courage to express our authentic voice and unwaveringly seek truth in a world that often drifts from it (Holiday, 2019).

In the grand tapestry of life, courage intertwines with our very essence, beckoning us to take bold steps toward our highest potential. With each courageous act, we inch closer to the extraordinary existence we envision. Awaken the deep reservoirs of courage within you and embrace the transformative power it holds. Embark on a journey of resolute action, facing challenges with unyielding determination, and let your inner courage radiate the path to a life of authenticity and fulfillment.

Justice

In the realm of Stoicism, justice, or *dikaiosyne*, transcends the mere framework of our legal system. It expands beyond laws and regulations, delving into treating everyone with unwavering respect, regardless of their background. This profound concept urges us to be mindful of our biases and unfair actions, inviting us to embody philanthropy and ethical conduct. Indeed, our moral obligation to others is intertwined with the fabric of justice.

The venerable Marcus Aurelius, the emperor and Stoic philosopher, regarded justice as the paramount virtue (Holiday, 2019). Its significance lies in being the foundation upon which all other virtues are built. He believed that justice should guide our external interactions with others and serve as an integral part of our character, fostering our personal fulfillment. Stoic justice entails not just the way we treat others but also how we treat ourselves. It beckons us to harmonize our choices with the greater good, embracing decisions that nurture long-term happiness while considering their impact on those around us.

To embark on this transformative path, we must embark on a journey of self-reflection, fearlessly exploring our biases and prejudices. By undertaking this inner examination, we pave the way toward fairness and equity in our dealings with others. Regardless of external factors, we are called upon to extend kindness and fairness to all, untethered to the actions of others. As Bastos (2022) eloquently puts it, it is about exuding kindness, respect, understanding, and generosity toward those in our midst. It entails offering unwavering support to those in need and embracing our role as contributors to the greater community rather than being mere recipients of its bounties.

Temperance

In Stoicism, the virtue of temperance, also known as *sophrosyne* or self-control, takes center stage. It is intricately intertwined with desire and seeks to establish a harmonious life balance. Rather than denying or completely indulging ourselves, temperance beckons us to embrace moderation and regulation in our desires and actions. It reminds us that a middle ground exists—a balanced "halfway" between what we yearn for and how we choose to conduct ourselves.

By embodying the virtue of temperance, we attain profound freedom—emancipation from the whims of our desires and passions. It empowers us to master ourselves, enabling rational decision-making and alignment with long-term well-being. When we integrate this virtue into our lives, it extends beyond material excesses. It invites us to examine the habits, routines, and mindful practices that support a virtuous existence (Holiday, 2019). Therefore, it becomes evident that temperance encompasses the realm of material indulgence and emotional moderation.

By cultivating emotional resilience and avoiding extreme reactions, we acquire the ability to make decisions rooted in clarity and reason. Stoic temperance emphasizes measured enjoyment and pleasure, recognizing that excesses can lead to discontentment and disrupt our inner harmony. By embracing moderation, we unearth a more profound sense of fulfillment that transcends external circumstances, shielding us from being carried away by the challenges we encounter. As The Collector (2022b) aptly states, the Stoics prioritized long-term well-being over short-term pleasures, which entails taking a step back and perceiving the bigger picture.

Core beliefs

Apart from the four virtues that you have just read about, Stoicism has three core beliefs upon which it is built. They refer to how we view life and how these will determine how we act, think, and pursue our happiness. They are the basis of the Stoic thought and, together with the four virtues, will determine the best action to take in each situation. In this section, we are going to take a look at what they are and how you can significantly change your life by incorporating them into it. They are the dichotomy of control; *amor fati*, or the love of fate; and *memento mori*, which is to remember our own mortality.

Dichotomy of control

The dichotomy of control relates directly to the core Stoic principle of what we can and cannot control. However, in this concept presented by the philosopher Epictetus, he makes it clear that the only things we do control are our thoughts and the voluntary actions that we make. "Everything else—such as our bodily sensations, the past, what other people think about us, and the outcome of our actions—is outside our direct control" (LeBon, 2023). Therefore, based on this principle, we should control what can be controlled and not try to do so with things that are uncontrollable.

Applying the principles of the dichotomy of control as teachers, we acknowledge that certain factors are beyond our influence. We cannot control the actions or circumstances of our students, nor can we alter biases or prejudices from individuals like crazy or mean school administrators (yes—you know—there are plenty of those around). Imagine a scenario in which a mean or irrational administrator gives us an unjustifiably negative evaluation after observing our lesson.

In such situations, the dichotomy of control becomes vital. While we cannot change the administrator's behavior, we have the power to choose our response. As Stoic educators, we face this challenge with serenity and wisdom. Instead of dwelling on the unfair evaluation, we focus on what we can control: our dedication to providing quality education and nurturing a positive learning environment for our students. We embody Stoic principles and resilience by maintaining our professionalism and focusing on their growth. We recognize that dwelling on the uncontrollable is fruitless; therefore, we invest our energy in what truly matters: the education and well-being of our students. Rest assured, the actions of an unprofessional administrator will ultimately lead to their own downfall, sooner or later.

Amor fati

The literal translation of this Stoic core belief is "the love of fate." This means that we should accept that things are as they are supposed to be. When you accept that things are as they should be, you will have the freedom to move on and avoid being frustrated, angry, depressed, and burned out. While it does not signify that you should accept everything as it is and become apathetic about life, it also means that you must focus on things that can be changed and are under your control. "Amor fati teaches unequivocal acceptance. Only then can you take control of it. Acceptance is a necessary precursor to change, an exercise in conserving your energy for what can be controlled, and leaving the rest" (Clarke, 2022).

Let's bring this into a context that relates to our routines as teachers. Suppose that you have a staff meeting every Wednesday afternoon after school and this is something that you do not look forward to. Not only are they not productive, but you could also be using your time for other things. When we use *amor fati*, we understand that these meetings will happen every Wednesday and there is nothing we can do to change that—it is an obligation and something that we have to attend. However, we can control and look at it from a different angle and try to make it more productive so that it brings positive outcomes. In this circumstance, you have something that you cannot change and must accept—the meeting—but you can also control how productive it will be based on suggestions and actions from both you and your peers.

Memento mori

In Book II, passage 17 of Marcus Aurelius's renowned *Meditations*, he imparts a pearl of timeless wisdom: "Death hangs over thee. While thou livest, while it is in thy power, be good" (C170 CE/2022). This profound maxim beckons us to embrace the belief of *memento mori*—a Stoic principle urging us to remember our mortality and the inevitable reality of death. By internalizing this concept, we cultivate an appreciation for life, finding joy and gratitude in its positive aspects. Recognizing the fleeting nature of existence, we are motivated to make the most of every moment, living our lives to the fullest. This approach unlocks a profound sense of well-being, enabling us to distance ourselves from negativity and embrace a positive outlook. Embracing the impermanence of life empowers us to seek fulfillment, embrace happiness, and savor the precious moments we are granted.

Death is inevitable, urging us to embrace the present. Find joy in your life, celebrate your students' achievements, and thrive in their participation. Cherish the camaraderie of fellow teachers who are your friends. Plan engaging activities that create lasting memories. These experiences can make a significant impact. Ask yourself: *If tomorrow were my last day, would I be content, knowing I've pursued happiness to the fullest?* Embrace the impermanence of life and seize every opportunity for fulfillment.

What teachers can learn from Stoic philosophy

In the public school system, such as the one we have in New York City, Stoic philosophy becomes an indispensable asset. To navigate and resist its challenges, one must embody the essence of a Stoic educator. Rather than merely seeking to guide our students onto a better path, we recognize that being part of this (sometimes absurd) system requires us to be Stoic philosophers already. Our inner strength, resilience, and adherence to Stoic principles allow us to endure and transcend obstacles. We embarked on a journey in this profession not solely out of a desire for personal fulfillment but to serve as catalysts for transformative change in the lives of our youth. Embracing Stoicism empowers us to embody these ideals and have a profound impact.

Furthermore, we must conceive that as educators, or especially Stoic educators, we are the ones responsible for showing these teenagers how they can develop through education. Barbosa (2020) mentions that for Epictetus, one of the most important philosophers of Stoicism, "each one of us is both teacher and student. We are all on a path of personal development, but this path is not linear; it is a spiral. You follow someone ahead of you and someone follows you in turn." Let me ask you: How many times have you learned from your students? I can tell you that, for me, this has been an exchange I have learned to appreciate: I teach the students and I also learn things from them.

And this is the first thing we can learn from the Stoics: to appreciate the small things that we have in life or, in our case, in school. We must learn to see the positive side of those who work with us, our students, other teachers, and everyone that is part of the education institution in which we are. It is essential that we learn how to celebrate all the achievements, big or small, and that we understand the part we have had in it. When was the last time you reflected on the impact you had on a student? You might not realize it because you were as tired and overwhelmed as I remember being.

This exhaustion that comes with the profession gives us the need to be strong, mentally tough, to overcome all the challenging situations we face. It is not uncommon to face mental challenges throughout our day, whether we are speaking to parents, colleagues, students, or the administration. We are usually responsible for solving conflicts that we were not taught how to handle, and it is up to us to learn how to do it. Therefore, having the mental fortitude of understanding the things you can and cannot control is essential for success on your journey as a teacher (Mepham, 2020).

It is important that we always remember that while we are teaching, we are exposed to the most diverse situations—people are not all the same, their circumstances change, and each one has a unique view and approach to life. Therefore, we must be ready and patiently guide our students and teach them based on what we believe and the values guiding our lives. It is about waiting for that perfect moment to seize the opportunity and use it as a teaching moment. That specific circumstance where you will be able to share some of your life experience.

Does it take time? Yes. Do I need to be patient? Certainly. Does this take some time to understand? Absolutely. But I believe that by presenting the tools in this book and sharing my experience with you, I can make this easier to understand. When you adopt a Stoic approach to teaching, you will build the resilience necessary to deal with difficult situations and have a more positive attitude even in the most challenging circumstances. We cannot control the school. We cannot control what other people will do. But we can choose the battles we will fight and how we will do so. And that, dear Stoic educator, is the secret to achieving a healthy approach to adversity.

Applying Stoic wisdom in Ms. Shern's classroom

Ms. Shern, a high school English teacher, faced disruptions from bright but distracted students Emily and Jake. Instead of reprimanding them, she applied Stoic wisdom—focusing on what she could control. She engaged them positively by giving them leadership roles during group activities and acknowledging their contributions. Over time, Emily and Jake, once a source of disruption, blossomed into responsible and valued members of the classroom. This transformation, brought about by Ms. Shern's wise approach, is a testament to the power of Stoic wisdom in the classroom.

This example vividly illustrates how wisdom allows educators to see beyond immediate frustrations and focus on long-term solutions. By understanding her students' deeper needs and motivations, Ms. Shern applied wisdom to foster a more harmonious and productive classroom environment. Her ability to pause, reflect, and make informed decisions based on the Stoic principles of wisdom made a significant impact. This impact, which led to a more positive and engaging classroom, underscores the long-term benefits of applying Stoic wisdom in education.

Teachers can truly harness the power of wisdom by embracing its guiding force to filter through the noise of daily challenges. It empowers them to separate profound insights that lead to a good life from the mere accumulation of data. Through the lens of wisdom, educators gain the precious gift of perspective, enabling them to make choices that align with their values and aspirations. By cultivating wisdom, teachers can transcend the superficial and access a profound understanding that leads to a well-lived life for themselves and their students. This empowerment is a key benefit of applying Stoic wisdom in the classroom.

Applying courage in the classroom: Mr. Thompson's stand

Mr. Thompson, a science teacher, faced a rigid curriculum policy stifling interactive learning. Courageously, he gathered evidence and advocated for a flexible, student-centered approach despite fears. Presenting a compelling case to the administration, he piloted interactive methods in his class. The undeniable positive outcomes in engagement and performance led the school to adopt a balanced curriculum incorporating interactive elements across subjects, thanks to Mr. Thompson's courageous efforts.

This example demonstrates how courage allows educators to stand up for what they believe is right, even in the face of adversity. Mr. Thompson's willingness to take purposeful action, despite the potential risks, ultimately led to positive change within the school. His courage not only benefited his students but also paved the way for a more enriching educational environment for the entire school.

Teachers can benefit from courage by embracing it as a guiding principle in their professional lives. By standing firm in their convictions and advocating for what is best for their students, educators can create meaningful and lasting change. Courage empowers teachers to act in alignment with their values, ensuring that their actions contribute to the greater good and foster a positive learning environment.

Courage is not merely about confronting fear; it is about taking resolute action in the face of adversity. As Stoic educators, we must cultivate this virtue, standing up for our principles and advocating for the well-being of our students. By doing so, we inspire our students to develop their own courage, creating a ripple effect that extends beyond the classroom.

Applying justice in the classroom: Ms. Martínez's inclusive classroom

Ms. Martínez, a dedicated elementary school teacher, encountered a formidable hurdle when Ahmed, a new student, joined her class in the middle of the academic year. Ahmed, a recent immigrant with limited English proficiency and a unique cultural background, was the center of attention. Ms. Martínez observed some students excluding Ahmed from group activities and making insensitive remarks about his language and culture.

Recognizing the significance of justice, Ms. Martínez empathetically decided to take action to ensure that Ahmed felt welcomed and respected. She began by reflecting on her biases and educating herself about Ahmed's cultural background. She also encouraged her students to share their cultural traditions, fostering an environment of mutual respect and understanding.

To further promote inclusivity, Ms. Martínez implemented several strategies:

- **Cultural appreciation day**: She organized a day where students could share food, stories, and customs from their cultures. This activity helped students appreciate the diversity within their classroom.

- **Peer support system**: She paired Ahmed with a buddy who helped him navigate the classroom and school routines. This not only supported Ahmed but also fostered empathy and leadership skills in his buddy.

- **Language inclusion**: Ms. Martínez incorporated basic words and phrases from Ahmed's language into daily classroom activities. This small gesture made Ahmed feel valued and helped other students understand the importance of communication and respect.

Over time, the classroom dynamic underwent a positive transformation. Students began to include Ahmed in their activities, and the insensitive comments ceased. Ahmed started to feel more confident and engaged in his learning, instilling a sense of hope and progress in the classroom.

This example illustrates how the virtue of justice can transform a classroom. By ensuring that every student is treated with respect and fairness, Ms. Martínez created an inclusive and supportive environment. Her actions went beyond enforcing rules; she actively worked to understand and address the underlying issues of exclusion and bias.

Teachers can benefit from justice by striving to create equitable learning environments. This involves recognizing and addressing biases, fostering mutual respect, and ensuring that all students feel valued and included.

By embodying the principles of justice, educators can profoundly inspire their students' lives, promoting a sense of belonging and respect that extends far beyond the classroom.

Justice is not a mere adherence to laws or rules; it's about cultivating an environment of fairness, respect, and inclusion. As Stoic educators, we must embody this virtue in our interactions with students, colleagues, and the broader school community. This commitment paves the way for a more just and equitable world, one classroom at a time.

Applying temperance in the classroom: Ms. Lee's balanced approach

Ms. Lee, a high school history teacher, often found herself overwhelmed by the myriad demands of her profession. Between grading assignments, preparing lessons, and managing classroom behavior, she struggled to maintain a sense of balance. She noticed that her stress levels were affecting her interactions with students, leading to frustration and impatience.

Realizing the need for a change, Ms. Lee decided to embrace the Stoic virtue of temperance. Stoicism is a philosophy that emphasizes the importance of self-control and moderation. She began by examining her daily routines and identifying areas where she could implement moderation and self-control. One significant change she made was setting boundaries for her work hours. Instead of grading papers late into the night, she allocated specific times during the day for grading and planning, ensuring that she had time to rest and recharge.

Ms. Lee also applied temperance in her emotional responses to classroom challenges. When faced with disruptive behavior, instead of reacting with immediate frustration, she practiced taking a deep breath and responding calmly. She reminded herself that she could not control her students' actions, but she could control her reactions. This approach allowed her to address issues with clarity and reason, maintaining a positive and supportive classroom environment.

Furthermore, Ms. Lee encouraged her students to practice temperance in their own lives. She integrated discussions on self-control and moderation into her history lessons, highlighting historical figures who exemplified these virtues. She also created opportunities for students to reflect on their own behaviors and set goals for balanced living.

This example illustrates how temperance can significantly impact a teacher's professional and personal life. By adopting a balanced approach, Ms. Lee was able to reduce her stress levels, improve her interactions with students, and create a more harmonious classroom environment. For instance, she found that when she responded calmly to disruptive behavior, students were more receptive to her guidance. Her commitment to temperance not only benefited her well-being but also served as a model for her students.

Temperance is not an abstract concept but a practical tool that can empower educators. By embracing moderation and self-control in their daily routines and emotional responses, teachers can make rational decisions, avoid burnout, and maintain a sense of inner harmony. This virtue is a key to creating a more balanced and fulfilling teaching experience, enhancing effectiveness and satisfaction in our roles.

Temperance is not just a personal virtue but a cornerstone of a positive classroom environment. It's about finding a balanced 'halfway' that supports long-term well-being. As Stoic educators, we must strive to embody this virtue, guiding our actions and reactions with moderation and self-control. By doing so, we not only nurture ourselves but also foster a culture of balance and fulfillment in our classrooms, benefiting our students and ourselves.

My journey with Stoicism

As a public school teacher, I realized that I had to be strong and resilient to deal with the challenges that come with the job in order to survive in such a chaotic and obsolete educational system. But it wasn't until I discovered the philosophy of Stoicism that I developed a positive mentality and the ability to handle anything that came my way.

I first learned about Stoicism while reading the works of Epictetus, Seneca, and Marcus Aurelius. Their teachings about focusing on what you can control and accepting what you cannot resonated deeply with me. I began to apply their principles in my personal life and, eventually, started to use them in my teaching.

When encountering challenging students, irate parents, high-pressure administrators, unscrupulous principals, discourteous payroll secretaries, or even school aides and paraprofessionals neglecting their responsibilities in the classroom, I constantly reminded myself to maintain composure and embrace the situation. Rather than becoming irritated or overwhelmed, I focused on improving circumstances. Gradually, I started perceiving these challenges as opportunities for personal growth and professional development rather than insurmountable obstacles.

Stoicism has been not just a philosophy I've studied but a transformative journey that has shaped my outlook on life. It has empowered me to maintain a positive attitude, even in the face of adversity, and to approach every situation with an open mind. It has instilled in me a sense of patience and understanding and a resilience that keeps me focused on my goals, even when the path is uncertain.

The Stoic philosophy has been a guiding light, providing a framework for navigating the complexities of life with grace and resilience. Its teachings have instilled a sense of inner calm and fortitude, enabling me to confront challenges head-on while maintaining a positive outlook.

The practical benefits of Stoicism in my professional life as a teacher have been profound. It not only has allowed me to approach my job with a positive mindset but also has given me a deeper sense of purpose and meaning in everything I do. Embracing Stoicism has shown me that embodying its teachings is a continuous journey filled with challenges, but the profound rewards it brings make every step worthwhile.

While the principles of Stoicism have proven invaluable in cultivating resilience and finding fulfillment in the noble teaching profession, the journey does not end here. The path of personal growth and self-mastery is an ongoing exploration, and the next chapter delves deeper into the practical application of Stoic wisdom in our daily lives.

In the next chapter, we will delve into the Stoic concept of distinguishing between what is within our control and what lies beyond our influence. This fundamental principle, once understood, can help us channel our energy and focus on the aspects of our lives that we can directly shape and impact.

Through practical exercises and real-life examples, we will delve into the Stoic concept of control and influence. This understanding will empower us to cultivate a mindset of acceptance and detachment toward external circumstances beyond our control while taking purposeful action within our sphere of influence. This powerful combination of wisdom and action will equip us to navigate life's challenges with greater clarity, resilience, and effectiveness.

As we delve into this transformative chapter, we will uncover strategies for identifying and expanding our sphere of influence, enabling us to make meaningful choices and create positive change in our personal and professional lives. Prepare to embark on a journey of self-discovery and personal growth, where the timeless teachings of Stoicism will serve as a compass, guiding us toward a life of purpose, fulfillment, and inner peace.

Bibliography

Barbosa, C. (2020, September 25). How should a Stoic look at education? *The Wise Mind.* Retrieved from https://thewisemind.net/how-should-a-stoic-look-at-education/

Bastos, F. (2022). The 4 Stoic virtues that will make you a better person. *Mind Owl.* Retrieved from https://mindowl.org/4-stoic-virtues/

Clarke, G. (2022, December 9). Finding amor fati through yoga: Amor fati meaning, love and accept your fate. *The Yoga Nomads.* Retrieved from https://www.theyoganomads.com/amor-fati-meaning/

Holiday, R. (2019, February 6). What is Stoicism? A definition & 9 Stoic exercises to get you started. *Daily Stoic.* Retrieved from https://dailystoic.com/what-is-stoicism-a-definition-3-stoic-exercises-to-get-you-started

LeBon, T. (2023, April 23). The Stoic dichotomy of control in practice. *Psychology Today.* Retrieved from https://www.psychologytoday.com/us/blog/365-ways-to-be-more-stoic/202304/the-stoic-dichotomy-of-control-in-practice

Mepham, J. (2020, November 11). What school leaders can learn from Stoic philosophy. *Headteacher Update.* Retrieved from https://www.headteacher-update.com/best-practice-article/what-school-leaders-can-learn-from-stoic-philosophy-headteachers/232082/

Mind of a Stoic. (n.d.). Stoic quotes. Retrieved from https://mindofastoic.com/stoic-quotes

Robertson, D. J. (2019, September 10). The Stoic virtues and code of honor. Medium; stoicism—philosophy as a way of life. Retrieved from https://medium.com/stoicism-philosophy-as-a-way-of-life/the-stoic-virtues-and-code-of-honor-2141ceae095f

Saunders, J. L. (2023, May 16). Stoicism. *Encyclopedia Britannica.* Retrieved from https://www.britannica.com/topic/Stoicism/Ancient-Stoicism

The Collector. (2022a, July 1). What are the origins of Stoicism? *The Collector.* Retrieved from https://www.thecollector.com/what-are-the-origins-of-stoicism-history/

The Collector. (2022b, July 5). What are the four cardinal virtues of Stoicism? *The Collector.* Retrieved from https://www.thecollector.com/what-are-the-four-cardinal-virtues-of-stoicism/

CHAPTER 2

Seizing Control

Mastering Your Sphere of Influence

DOI: 10.4324/9781003535652-3

6 6 Some things are within our power, while others are not. Within our power are opinion, motivation, desire, aversion, and, in a word, whatever is of our own doing; not within our power are our body, our property, reputation, office, and, in a word, whatever is not of our own doing.

Epictetus, *Enchiridion*

One of the most challenging things I had to learn as a teacher was that there were things I could not control and things weren't always going to go the way I planned or wanted them to. Whether it was concerning a student's behavior in class or the response of the administration secretary to my requests, I learned I had to accept things that were beyond my control. This was not as easy as I thought it would be.

In the beginning, before I came in contact with Stoic philosophy, I thought that it was up to me to take matters into my own hands and "make them right." I bet you can relate to the feeling. It usually happens to us when we are beginning, and we have no idea of what to expect from the public school environment. Once again, we are not taught this in university. We are not given tools to deal with what we go through every day. We are *not prepared* to deal with the adversity we are going to face. No one tells us what it is going to be like.

We are just expected to "go and teach." No one tells us that teachers will have to deal with students who come from a challenging background or that if you start to make positive changes, you will be the target of your colleagues. We aren't given lessons on how to deal with conflict or how to manage the more than complex educational system that exists—bureaucracy, war of egos, and so much more.

However, once I learned that I simply *could not* control everything and that I should focus on *what I did have the power over*, things started to change. When I understood that I could still navigate challenges with the tools I developed and "go around" the system, things started to look up. I then had a new understanding on how to approach these situations that had been demanding so much from me mentally and led me to feel tired and burned out. I saw that *I had chosen* to suffer from these situations, because I decided to let them affect me.

What changed? you might ask. I began to understand that there were simply things I could not change—I could not get involved in a student's personal family matters; I wasn't going to stop people from gossiping about my teaching methods—there was simply no way to control it all. I came to the conclusion that, if I was going to try to control everything, that would lead me to become even more distressed and demotivated to continue teaching. This was when I adopted the Stoic belief of the dichotomy of control; I started to think about the things I could change rather than the things I could not. How I could, in fact, make a change based on the things that were within my reach.

If a student was misbehaving in class because they were having family problems, I would speak to them and try to show empathy and a welcoming environment in school—listen to them. If I was having trouble with school material that did not arrive, I would do my best to provide the materials I needed to carry out the class. I started *preparing* better, both my material and my mind, for what I would have to deal with in school. I decided that I could not change where I worked but that I could, and should, change my approach to these issues. I developed an internal *locus* of control.

Develop an internal locus of control

The term *locus of control* was developed by the psychologist Julian B. Rotter in 1954 and became one of the most popular theories regarding human behavior. According to this theory, this *locus* could be either "internal (a conviction that one can handle one's own life) or external (a conviction that life is constrained by outside factors which the individual can't impact or that possibility or destiny controls their lives)" (Lopez-Garrido, 2023). As you can see, since it is about how one perceives one's life situations, this principle is strongly related to the Stoic principles of dichotomy of control and *amor fati*.

When you have an external locus of control, you will have an approach of acceptance to things in life with a certain apathy. This means that those who have this characteristic wait for things to happen to them and do not react. They believe there is nothing they can do about ongoing situations. Essentially speaking, they take *amor fati* to its most passive instance and let fate decide how things will play out. However, as we have already seen in the previous chapter, acceptance *does not* equal apathy. And this is where the dichotomy of control comes in.

An individual who has an internal locus of control believes that they make things happen and they can control certain things in their lives. This means they understand certain events cannot be changed, but nevertheless they are determined to take control of what they can. Generally speaking, those who have an internal locus of control will usually take matters into their own hands when they see the opportunity.

Let's put this into a practical example. Suppose you have a student who is not performing well in class. You then discover it is because they are facing some difficulties at home. Obviously, you cannot interfere with their lives or meddle in their personal business. However, you can offer to the whole class (not to exclude them) to give some extra tutoring lessons for all the students who feel they need help. While you cannot control what is going on at home, you can make yourself available to them in another way.

However, it will be up to the student to decide if they want to show up after class or not. You *can* control your schedule and give additional lessons. But you cannot force them to show up or be interested in learning or obtaining help. In this case, you have *accepted* their circumstance, because there is nothing you can do to change what is going on at home. However, you have *taken action* in making yourself available for extra tutoring time, which is something you can control. What they will do is up to them; this is also something you cannot control.

Win more battles

If I have to accept circumstances and focus on what I can control, does that mean I should recognize defeat? That nothing can change? Well, something like that. You know that popular saying "pick your battles"? It is more or less what you will have to do here. The only difference being that you focus on the things which you can change. This means there is no use worrying about situations you cannot control. Think about the things that are within your reach—big or small. Is there anything you can do to change them? What would you do if you were given the possibility to take action?

I want you to do a small mental exercise here. I want you to think about the ten things that are most distressing to you in the school environment, no matter the size. List the things that bother you. Once you have done this, I want you to go back and analyze each situation: is there anything you can do to change them? Is modifying them something you have the power to do? If the answer is "no," then you already know what you must do. However, if the answer is "yes," I would like you to consider the possibility of *doing something* and being the agent of change.

In this list you have made, there are probably things you cannot change—it is likely that those make up most of the list. Outdated material, missing supplies, no infrastructure, attitude or ego problems with colleagues or students, and even lack of support from the administration. Yes, I know. We have all been there at one time or the other. You are so tired that you will look at this list and think, *Well, I have tried everything, there is not much more that I can do.*

But I want you to give it a second thought. You cannot control the missing supplies (or the lack of budget to help with that), but could you come up with more recent material? Maybe something that you found on your own? Maybe printed copies that the students could use? This could be a way around the situation. You don't have support from the administration, but you have a teacher colleague with whom you work really well. Maybe you could suggest a project with both subjects. Think about this. I can bet that if you give it some thought and add a bit of creativity, there are plenty of ways to get around certain situations—possibilities you haven't thought of.

When you think about the challenging situations you face day in and day out, or even look at the quick list you have just made, you will see there are things that will be easier to do and things that will be harder. In this case, you must analyze and decide which battle you want to fight. Which will bring you the fastest outcome? Although you might want to make changes to all the items on the list, I suggest you start with the things that will bring you a faster and greater sense of accomplishment. The reason for this is that completing these actions will give you a boost in energy and keep your motivation high. If you feel the effort to win the battle will demand too much from you, you can let it go and accept it or come up with alternative solutions.

One of the most refreshing ways to navigate the challenges of each day is to unleash your creativity and embrace unconventional thinking. By exploring different possibilities, you equip yourself with the tools to triumph over unexpected hurdles or battles that arise. However, educators often overlook another practice, a secret weapon that can ignite inspiration and bring joy to the classroom. What is it? If you said, "Embrace the power of silliness," you're right! Embracing laughter and whimsy in your lessons captivates students and infuses your teaching with contagious energy. It opens up new avenues for engagement and cultivates an atmosphere of lighthearted learning. So, when you plan your lessons for the next day, week, or beyond, remember to sprinkle in a touch of laughter and a dash of playfulness and watch as your students' enthusiasm soars. Embracing the power of silliness is essential to conquering battles and transforming adversity into triumph.

Preparing yourself for the next teaching day

Have you ever encountered the misconception that teachers work only during class hours? We both know that our dedication extends far beyond the confines of the 8–3 schedule. There's grading, meetings, and, of course, the crucial aspect of preparation. Planning is a cornerstone of effective teaching. As you engage with your students today, your thoughts extend to tomorrow's lesson and how it relates to their long-term understanding. If you find yourself neglecting this crucial step, the truth is you're unintentionally paving a path toward challenges and potential setbacks. Preparation is the key to success, ensuring you're equipped to inspire and empower your students most effectively.

Let me emphasize this undeniable truth: planning is an inseparable part of the teaching journey. It is not merely a recommended practice; it is an essential one. Rarely will you find a teacher stepping into a classroom without a clear idea of what they will impart and how they will navigate potential obstacles. However, despite thorough preparation, there are instances where even our best efforts could be better. If you are within your initial three years of teaching, consider this a golden chance to embrace the profound benefits of meticulous planning, laying the foundation for future triumphs. Prepare diligently, for it is through strategic planning that we pave the way for a rewarding educational experience.

Preparation takes time, research, creative thinking, and imagining the different outcomes that a lesson will have. For example, if you are teaching something that is content-heavy, you might want to come up with an activity to help lighten the mood. Maybe this activity could help the students absorb the material that they saw in class more easily. Since you are well versed in the subject you are teaching, it is more than likely you know where the struggles will be and where the most doubts will be present. If you can anticipate this, the probability you will be able to help your students if they struggle during the lesson is higher.

Once you see that you *were* able to reasonably foresee where the problems were and where they found the subject challenging, it will be possible to adequately prepare future lessons. When you do this, your students will thrive because you are already altering the way you teach to better suit your class. As you gain more experience, you will see that some approaches work for some classes or students but not for others. Nevertheless, because you have spent time planning and preparing, you will have a full toolkit of options, making you feel more confident about the final outcome of the lesson. Better yet, you will have a whole list of options that will even help you maintain the discipline of the class and their attention while you are speaking.

Embrace the liberating truth: you need not surrender to the status quo simply because you perceive no escape. When faced with rigid curriculum or school policies, infuse your unique touch. Seek alternatives and gather perspectives. Remember, reinventing the wheel is unnecessary. The internet is a treasure trove of educational resources, a beacon of inspiration. Countless brilliant ideas crafted by fellow teachers await your discovery. Borrow, adapt, and implement them in your classroom, breathing fresh life into your teaching practice. Let the collective wisdom of educators fuel your creativity and innovation. Explore, learn, and make these valuable resources your own.

Finally, remember that, in the classroom, you *do control* the lesson. So, plan it by thinking about which objectives you are trying to reach. How you are going to do that? Save some time for essential student hands-on activities or practice. See if there are any learning aids you can use and other additional material you can share (Mutaawe, 2022). Lastly, keep in mind that you should be *resilient*, which we will talk more about in the coming chapter. If things don't go the way you planned, be prepared to bounce back, review your plans, and change what is needed. The lesson and the classroom are things you can control, so use them to your advantage!

Learning to control reactions

As a teacher, I have learned that sometimes the best approach to a difficult situation is to focus on what I can control. The Stoic principle of focusing on what is within our control helps deal with toxic problems in my school.

For example, a payroll secretary repeatedly failed to submit my paperwork for after-school activities, leaving me unpaid for weeks on end. I knew I couldn't control her actions, but I could control my response. I approached her with kindness and understanding rather than anger and frustration. By focusing on what I could control, I worked to build a more positive relationship with her, and, surprisingly, she started submitting my paperwork on time.

Another instance was when I had an assistant principal who did not value the importance of Spanish in the school. He refused to provide me with enough textbooks for all of my classes. Instead of becoming angry and aggressive, I focused on what I could control. I worked with other teachers to find alternative resources and materials for my students and even created my own materials. This allowed me to continue providing quality instruction for my students, even when faced with a difficult situation.

However, it was also under my control to inform the principal of the situation. Telling the principal did not help at all. Realizing it was also under my control to contact the superintendent, I sent an email explaining how our students, for months, did not have textbooks and depended on photocopies I marvelously managed to make for them daily (teachers could not make photocopies either—the copier at the teachers' office did not work and the only other copier available had a code that the administration refused to give teachers), and guess what? The books were delivered two days after I sent the email. Not only that but the copier in the teachers' lounge was also fixed. My colleagues and

I could now make copies for our students without going through all those hierarchical steps to find someone who knew the code and was willing to make copies for us.

This anecdote exemplifies the transformative impact of embracing our sphere of influence. By recognizing the aspects of the situation that were within our control (such as contacting the superintendent) and taking purposeful action, we were able to catalyze positive change and overcome seemingly insurmountable obstacles. The delivery of textbooks and restoring the copier in the teachers' lounge were tangible victories. Still, the true triumph lies in the realization that we possess the power to shape our circumstances when we focus on what is within our control.

Through these experiences, I have learned that focusing on what we can control can help us remain calm and positive and find creative solutions to problems. This valuable lesson in resilience, the ability to bounce back from adversity, has helped me in my personal and professional life.

Undoubtedly, the ability to discern and act upon our sphere of influence is a priceless skill that transcends the boundaries of any single domain. By cultivating this mindset, we not only equip ourselves with the resilience and resourcefulness to navigate life's challenges but also foster a sense of accomplishment and optimism. We find creative solutions, maintain a positive outlook even in the face of adversity, and emerge stronger on the other side.

While mastering our sphere of influence is a potent tool, it is important to remember that the journey of personal growth and self-mastery is not a destination but a continuous process. In the next chapter, "The Art of Resilience: Thriving in the Face of Adversity," we will delve into the heart of the Stoic philosophy, exploring the principles and practices that enable us to endure and thrive in the face of life's inevitable challenges. This ongoing journey is a testament to our perseverance and commitment to personal growth.

Resilience is not merely a passive state of endurance; it is an active, dynamic process that requires cultivating a specific mindset and developing practical skills. Through this chapter, we will uncover the secrets to building emotional fortitude, maintaining perspective, and finding meaning and purpose despite adversity.

Prepare to embark on a transformative journey. We will learn to reframe our perception of challenges, embrace the growth opportunities they present, and develop a deep sense of inner strength and equanimity. By mastering the art of resilience, each of us will emerge as a beacon of hope and inspiration, capable of weathering life's storms with grace and emerging stronger on the other side.

Bibliography

Big Think. (n.d.). CBT and Stoicism: How ancient philosophy is at the heart of modern therapy. Retrieved from https://bigthink.com/neuropsych/cbt-stoicism/

Daily Stoic. (n.d.). What is Stoicism? A definition & 3 Stoic exercises to get you started. Retrieved from https://dailystoic.com/what-is-stoicism-a-definition-3-stoic-exercises-to-get-you-started/#what-is-stoicism

Daily Stoic. (n.d.). The 4 Stoic virtues. Retrieved from https://dailystoic.com/4-stoic-virtues/

Headteacher Update. (n.d.). What school leaders can learn from stoic philosophy. Retrieved from https://www.headteacher-update.com/best-practice-article/what-school-leaders-can-learn-from-stoic-philosophy-head-teachers/232082/

Jedrew, S. (n.d.). A brief history of stoicism. Retrieved from https://www.simonjedrew.com/a-brief-history-of-stoicism/

Lopez-Garrido, G. (2023, February 8). Locus of control theory in psychology: Definition & examples. *Simply Psychology*. Retrieved from https://www.simplypsychology.org/locus-of-control.html

Mutaawe, A. (2022, August 31). 8 things you should prepare before your next teaching day. *Teacher.ac*. Retrieved from https://teacher.ac/8-things-you-should-prepare-before-your-next-teaching-day/

Orion Philosophy. (n.d.). What is Stoicism? Retrieved from https://www.orionphilosophy.com/stoic-blog/what-is-stoicism

Orion Philosophy. (n.d.). The 4 Stoic virtues. Retrieved from https://www.orionphilosophy.com/stoic-blog/4-stoic-virtues

The Collector. (n.d.). What are the origins of stoicism? *History*. Retrieved from https://www.thecollector.com/what-are-the-origins-of-stoicism-history/

The Collector. (n.d.). What is Stoicism? The Stoics' beliefs. Retrieved from https://www.thecollector.com/what-is-stoicism-the-stoics-beliefs/

CHAPTER 3

The Art of Resilience

Thriving in the Face of Adversity

DOI: 10.4324/9781003535652-4

❝ Be tolerant with others and strict with yourself.

Marcus Aurelius, *Meditations*

It is essential that we, as teachers, learn how to recover quickly from the adverse situations we face—there is always another class to teach or another issue requiring our urgent attention. Once you are able to do this, you can say that you have developed *resilience*. Think about it as a rubber band: after being stretched, it still goes back to its original state. This is what is usually required of us, and sometimes, no matter how hard we try, we just cannot bounce back.

One of the main things that some people fail to understand is that we *have a life* outside school. This means that, apart from dealing with all the daily challenges within the educational institution, we have private lives we must care for. Some of us have children, spouses, families, and friends we would like to dedicate attention to, and we cannot because of the overwhelming situations bothering us in the classroom.

Acknowledge the truth: it is undeniable that our classroom emotions often spill over into our personal lives—a relatable experience for many. Consequently, it becomes imperative to cultivate the mental fortitude and resilience discussed in this chapter. A vital aspect of this process lies in mastering emotional management. We must learn to rein in the immediate impulses that arise when anger, frustration, or nervousness strikes. The Stoics offer valuable insights on navigating these challenges. By acquiring the skill of emotional regulation, we empower ourselves to respond thoughtfully rather than impulsively. This vital pursuit forms a core theme in the Stoic teachings we will explore.

Stoicism and emotions

When we talk about the Stoic approach to emotions, the common belief that adepts of the philosophy must refrain from feeling any emotion leaps to the minds of most people. However, let me tell you this is not at all accurate. Rather than teaching the individual not to feel, Stoicism talks about the need to control and regulate these feelings so they do not interfere with your actions. Seneca once said, "It's OK to be surprised. It's OK to be scared. No amount of philosophy can remove that initial feeling, but what you can work towards is getting to a place where you're not ruled by these things" (Daily Stoic, 2021).

This does not mean you won't feel anger, or happiness, or love, for example. It just means you will learn to manage the *impulse* your body will immediately have as soon as it starts experiencing them. And you know what? It is completely normal to react. It is normal and only *human* to be this way. It was how our ancestors lived and how they were able to survive challenging and dangerous situations. However, it is important that you learn to understand where your negative emotions come from and how you can find a solution to make them go away.

In this situation, the Stoics embraced two complementary approaches for managing emotions: involuntary experiences and conscious rationalization. Through this process, you will develop the ability to acknowledge and accept your feelings. When you feel your nerves being triggered or an overwhelming urge to react when confronted with injustice, you instinctively respond to what your body perceives as a potential threat. These risks can manifest in physical, mental, or social forms. The ancient Stoics regarded these reactions as neutral—devoid of inherent goodness or badness—and as the body's natural response to danger (Orion Philosophy, 2020).

Are you stressed or frustrated because your class is misbehaving? Possibly, in this case, this is a natural reaction to the risk of being disrespected and not taken seriously by your students. It is only natural that you will feel nervous and distressed, that your body is going to react somehow because of the way you feel. But what should you do? According to the Stoics, you accept this is how you feel, but do not act on it. *Acceptance* is the first step to knowing how to deal with emotions.

After accepting what you are feeling, you are going to examine *why*. This is important because it will give you the root cause and help you take the next step, which is to do something about it. While the feelings you are experiencing are not something you can control, they are our body's automatic response; you can decide if and how you are going to act on them.

This is when the Stoic virtues of courage and wisdom will come into practice. You will need the wisdom to consider the situation that you are going through and, with courage, determine if it is something you are willing to stand up for. You must remember that, according to the Stoics, it is essential that we take a stand concerning our beliefs and what we think is the correct action to take. We must also remember that *withholding action* can also be a sign of courage and sometimes of self-preservation.

Being resilient

*B*ut how will I know if I am resilient enough? Well, this is an excellent question. This will require that you dive into self-analysis, examining how you react to certain situations and how fast you are able to recover from them. Whether they are internal or external situations, you must look deep within yourself and see how distressing and challenging situations affect you and if you let your emotions take you over or not.

Suppose that you are facing a common situation in school: the lack of appropriate material to teach. Here, you have two options: the first is to complain about it, pout, and spread the negativity affecting you in the class, giving negative feelings to others throughout the day. The second is to take action and see that, since the school administration is not willing to help you, you will need to come up with solutions on your own. This does not mean you are not upset about the situation. But it does mean you are going to "bounce back" from the negative situation you are facing, and instead of letting negative feelings dominate and impact your classes, you are going to turn it into something positive.

If you are able to do this—manage your feelings and the actions you take—and prevent an adverse event from taking over and upsetting you, it is likely you are a resilient person. At least, more resilient than other people who would just not react. Here, can you see how there is a common link between the core beliefs of dichotomy of control and *amor fati* with the virtues of courage, wisdom, temperance, and the skill of being resilient? Even though we are looking at it from different angles, it all goes back to these Stoic principles.

Now, I don't want you to worry if you think you are not as resilient, because sometimes it can happen that we are more resilient in some things than others. "You might demonstrate a lot of resilience when it comes to one challenge you're faced with, but struggle more with being resilient when it comes to another stressor you're up against" (Hurley, 2022). Looking at it from this point of view, you should understand that you might be a resilient person in your personal life, for example, but that you need to develop this skill for the classroom.

It is likely that, because you are in school most of the time and there are stressors that you cannot foresee or prevent, you will have to practice more when you are in the classroom. And let me be honest: it won't be immediate. Learning how to be resilient does not happen overnight, and it is something we always need to improve, especially in this fast-paced world that always presents us with new challenges. In addition to this, it would be impossible for me to tell you the exact formula to become more resilient—this is personal and complex and will depend exclusively on each individual's environment, personality, strengths, and weaknesses (Hurley, 2022).

This means there is no easy way out—life will present hardships, and you cannot overcome them without confronting them. This is the only way to build resilience. Running away from the things that demand your attention or your focus is not going to help you. Avoidance is simply not an option if you feel you need to build your resilience. In fact, avoidance is almost the opposite of resilience and controlling your emotions since you are literally giving in to the feelings of fear and unhappiness and showing apathy toward life.

Owing to our unique experiences, there is no single way to teach resilience, so a pediatrician named Ken Ginsburg developed the seven Cs of resilience for children and young adults (Hurley, 2022). These are important because teaching your students to be resilient can also lead to a more positive school environment. It might help prevent conflict and lead them to understand they need to control what they can. When you are a Stoic educator, you should use your wisdom and teaching methods to ensure that you are giving them, and yourself, the chance to become more resilient to the situations that life will bring.

According to CBT Professionals (2013), we could summarize the seven Cs of resilience in the following manner:

- **Competence**: How skilled you are in dealing with challenging situations and how easily you can overcome the difficulties you face. This ability is developed over time, with practice, after being exposed to adversity, thus making you feel competent in tackling them.

- **Confidence**: Having the confidence to deal with difficult situations is directly linked to how skilled you believe you are in dealing with them. Thus, the importance of practicing and being exposed to adversity. The more you are required to find solutions on your own, the better you will become at it, giving you more confidence for future issues.

- **Connection**: When you feel you belong to a social circle, it is more probable you will be resilient to different situations. The reason for this is that having support and people you can rely on will make you feel secure. When you strengthen your sense of belonging to a certain group—of friends, family, coworkers, or even a neighborhood group—you gain strong values and it prevents you from engaging in negative action.

- **Character**: When you have a strong personality, it almost instantly means that you are a confident person. It is believed that people with strong character will be able to make wiser decisions and differentiate between right and wrong more easily than others. You will know what you want, and likely have a strong sense of justice and self-knowledge, enabling you to use your wisdom to guide others.

- **Contribution**: People who continually contribute to helping the world become a better place can be considered more resilient. This means they will look for opportunities to bring joy and happiness and to get away from negative feelings. When you contribute and there is a positive outcome, you are also making yourself more confident in your actions and enhancing your competence.

- **Coping**: If you have the correct tools to learn how to cope with the distresses and challenging situations you are presented with, it is likely you will be more resilient. You will have a different skill set that will enable you to face even the most demanding situations with ease, thus reducing the stress levels and the negative consequences of certain issues.

- **Control**: Lastly, we need to consider control as a way of being resilient. When you are in control of your feelings, your actions, and your thoughts, you more easily understand and examine the real issue and make assertive decisions. When you are in control of what you are doing, you more easily rebound from adverse situations and regain your balance.

While these are all characteristics that we may have or might need to work on, it is helpful to understand everything that helps us build resilience. We are now going to look at the other things that you can do in order to develop this skill. In addition to this, we are going to look at how developing Stoic mental toughness will help you navigate difficult situations. And to do this, we are going to look into another class of professionals who are constantly challenged in a demanding and misunderstood area of work: athletes.

Developing Stoic mental toughness and resilience

When you think about the mental preparation that an athlete has to endure, you might find it pretty amazing what they are able to do: participating in intense competitions, dealing with a public who can be for or against them, and coping with extreme competition with other professionals. However, this is not how they are usually *perceived* by fans or those who are watching.

Just like us teachers, all people see are the athletes in their area of performance, which in our case is the classroom. No one follows their day-long training sessions, the things they must give up to compete if they want to be successful. This also happens to us when we are preparing lessons away from the eyes of the students, administration, and colleagues. People do not see how much effort we put into our lessons when we could be with our loved ones. In both instances, all they see is the end result, without thinking about what comes "in between."

In an interview, mental performance coach Seth Haselhuhn, a Stoic follower, mentions several points that could be useful to our teaching lives. To him, "mental performance is about being prepared, staying focused on the moment, and trying to predict the future" (Holiday, 2018). Now, does this remind you of anything you have read recently? Can you relate what Haselhuhn is saying to the Stoic values and principles you have just read about? I bet you can! And you can do this because the principle of mental toughness and resilience can be adopted into the life of any professional—from teachers, to businesspeople, to athletes.

The first thing you should know is that every outcome, of every situation, everything you do, everything you can control, will depend exclusively on your preparation, effort, and determination to make it happen (Simply Psychology, n.d; Soulsalt, n.d). And this is not just something you learn and then stop because you have reached your maximum potential. No, it is something that will keep taking you to the next level, when you deal with issues that are more and more challenging. The more effort you make to improve, learn, and develop, the better your results will be.

However, to achieve this, you must focus on your goals. Do you want a better teaching environment? Think about the ways you can bring positive change. You want a better-behaved class? Think about ways you can approach them and get their attention so they do not become distracted during the lesson. Being determined and focusing on solving the matter (remember: that you can control) will give you the extra push in the effort you need to make. "Focus is our ability to direct our attention to what is relevant and ignore what isn't. Concentration is our ability to focus over time. Know what's important, right now" (Holiday, 2018).

And how might I know what I should focus on? That is a very good question. The best way to do this is to set goals. Ask yourself, what are your objectives? What is it you want to achieve? What is it you want to accomplish? Once you have the answer to these questions, it will enable you to establish your short- and long-term goals (Mind Tools). When you establish what you want, it is easier to draw the path to take you there. You will be able to determine what the unexpected events are that may occur, what challenges you are likely to face, and what needs to be done to reach the best outcome.

Finally, you need to visualize what it is that you want. A great part of this includes talking to yourself. Most of us tend to listen—to the intrusive thoughts, the negative feelings, and the distressing situations. We are immediately taken to the worst-case scenario in our minds, leading us to think about the possible disastrous consequences to our actions. This is not the way to go. You must stop listening to what your mind is telling you as a result of years of thinking about the negative and start *telling yourself* what can be done. Instead of listening to the thoughts saying you can't do it, tell them you can, and you will. Visualize the solution.

Furthermore, it is important you have the path drawn for you so you can understand what threats you are going to face and find the meaning to what you are doing. Think about it with me: why would you engage in certain actions if they have no meaning to you? It might be related to the virtue of justice, for example, but it has to have a more significant purpose. It is important you understand the value of the things you do and those that you are going to do. Once you have this, it will be easier to solve problems.

Here, let me be sure that you understand what I mean: finding answers is easy, anyone can come up with a solution to a problem. Anyone who takes five minutes to reflect on a situation can come up with an alternative. However, how many of these people are willing to *act* on the proposed solution and make it effective, make it real? This is the difference between people who are resilient and those who are not or between those who have mental toughness and those who do not. They practice. They don't just think about finding answers to problems, they also take action to solve them. However, you will be able to determine what you should do in each situation only based on your own experience and wisdom, even if that means not taking action at all.

Dealing with adversity

While grading papers in the school library, I was interrupted by a student cursing loudly on the phone. The disruption started attracting attention, so I approached the student and politely asked him to lower his voice. Instead of complying, he started cursing at me, perhaps to provoke a reaction.

At that moment, I remembered the teachings of Stoic philosophy and chose to remain calm and patient. I didn't argue back or force him to be quiet. Instead, I walked away and tried to focus on my work while contemplating a creative solution.

As the angry student stormed out of the library, I heard the librarian confronting him at the entrance. He continued to act out, yelling and even throwing things off her desk. It was heart-breaking to watch; it was an unforgivable scenario. However, I knew my decision not to react was an example of handling difficult situations with resilience and grace.

In that moment, the choice to remain composed and refrain from reacting impulsively was a powerful demonstration of the resilience cultivated through the teachings of Stoicism. It was a testament to the ability to maintain perspective, even in the face of provocation, and to respond with wisdom rather than emotion.

As teachers, we are often expected to hand down discipline, to call out bad behavior and disruptions. However, more than 20 years of experience in New York City classrooms has taught me that, sometimes, it's better to allow our intuition to guide us, listen—really listen—and not react impulsively. It can be challenging, but sometimes the best action is to follow the flow and trust our instincts.

The role of an educator is multifaceted, and while maintaining discipline is a crucial aspect, true wisdom lies in recognizing when a situation calls for a different approach. Through years of experience, the art of resilience has revealed itself not only in the ability to endure challenges but also in the discernment to respond with empathy, patience, and a deep understanding of the human condition.

While the principles of Stoicism and the cultivation of resilience have proven invaluable in navigating the complexities of the teaching profession, it would be naive to assume that the path is without its unique challenges and struggles. In the next chapter, we will delve into the harsh realities and obstacles that educators often face, shedding light on the trials and tribulations that test the mettle of even the most resilient among us.

We will explore the multifaceted challenges that educators encounter, from navigating bureaucratic hurdles and managing limited resources to dealing with disruptive behavior, parental conflicts, and the emotional toll of the profession. This chapter will serve as a poignant reminder of the sacrifices and dedication required to shape the minds of future generations.

Bibliography

CBT Professionals. (2013, December 14). The 7 C's of resilience. *CBT Professionals*. Retrieved from https://cbtprofessionals.com.au/the-7-cs-of-resilience

Daily Stoic. (2021). Stoic quotes. *Daily Stoic*. Retrieved from https://dailystoic.com/stoic-quotes/

Holiday, R. (2018, March 26). How to develop Stoic mental toughness and resilience: Interview with coach Seth Haselhuhn. *Daily Stoic*. Retrieved from https://dailystoic.com/seth-haselhuhn/

Hurley, K. (2022, July 14). What is resilience? Your guide to facing life's challenges, aversities, and crises. *Everyday Health*. Retrieved from https://www.everydayhealth.com/wellness/resilience/

Mind Tools. (n.d.). Locus of control. Retrieved from https://www.mindtools.com/pages/article/newCDV_90.htm

Orion Philosophy. (2020, March 17). What do Stoics think about emotions? Medium; Orion Philosophy. https://medium.com/@orion_philosophy/what-do-stoics-think-about-emotions-orion-philosophy-2c230a15a37c

Simply Psychology. (n.d.). Locus of control. Retrieved from https://www. simplypsychology.org/locus-of-control.html

SoulSalt. (n.d.). Focus on what you can control. Retrieved from https:// soulsalt.com/focus-on-what-you-can-control/

CHAPTER 4
Struggles of an Educator

DOI: 10.4324/9781003535652-5

❝ We are more often frightened than hurt; and we suffer more in imagination than in reality.

Seneca, *Letters from a Stoic*

We have most certainly all had our struggles in the classroom—who hasn't? In the university, they do not teach us how to manage a class. We are not taught how to deal with disobedient students who challenge us on a daily basis and make us just want to give up. If you have ever felt like this, don't worry, you are not alone. In the beginning of my career, I often felt the same—that is, until I was able to come up with my own strategy for dealing with classroom issues that came up every day.

Going on the internet to find strategies to solve problems might seem like a solution, right? However, with just a simple search of the keywords "classroom management," you will find over 500 million results, which is quite amazing. That is an overwhelming number, and it just shows that everyone has a tactic, an opinion, or a suggestion on how you should deal with your unruly students.

But before we get into some of the tools I will give you to develop a technique that works for *you*, I want to first talk a little about some of the most common challenges we need to face—ranging from students who have problems at home and bring them to school, to those who challenge you for control; the list goes on and on. There always seems to be something new going on or a different way they manage to have us wanting to crawl under our sheets and stay there.

Classroom management

The first thing you should know, and I want to make this very clear, is that *it is not your fault*. It is impossible to control the external circumstances that affect our students or what they are thinking. Therefore, I don't want you to feel bad because of something that you were not taught how to deal with or if you still haven't found your way to dealing with the issue; this is what I am here for: to help you do this! Essentially speaking, there are certain skills you can develop that will make you walk into a classroom and show them that things *can* be different but that their attitude in the classroom must change.

Some of the biggest issues we see in students who misbehave include acting out because they want attention or are frustrated about something; the need to control the classroom; the desire to get revenge on someone, or something, because of what is going on in their lives; and, finally, boredom (Ashleigh, 2019). This does not mean that you have poor classroom management—not at all. These issues are more to do with the students than with you. You should remember that they also have a life outside school, and sometimes, they are going through things that we can't even imagine.

For this reason, one of the first things I suggest you do is try to improve this relationship by establishing communication. Once you start speaking to them, to try to better understand what is going on, you will see that it will make managing the classroom in general easier, especially if they are one of the "leaders" among the students. However, let me warn you that this does not mean you should confront them. It means showing you are open to dialogue and to helping them surpass what is going on so they can focus on their learning.

Banks (2020) suggests that what every teacher should do, although it can be exhausting, is to find the root cause of the misbehavior. These root causes can range from their basic needs (such as being fed or getting enough rest) not being met to relationship problems with family members and friends and even medical issues. Most of the time, these students will seek out attention as a way to feel heard or seen—and this leads to bad classroom behavior. When this happens, "when they want something or don't want something, they act out. While it can be hard to be strong in the face of inappropriate behavior, it's a must" (Banks, 2020).

When this happens, most of us who lack experience just give up and back down, refusing to reinforce the classroom rules. However, that only makes it worse. This is because when we back down and adjust to what they want, we are just reinforcing this bad attitude. We are literally telling them that their bad behavior got them somewhere. And if that happens, why would they change their attitude? It would make no sense—they are already achieving the desired effect!

And you know what? That makes us tired and unwilling to work on our classroom management skills. It demotivates us because we are unable to do what we have been hired and taught to do, which is teach. It seems as if everything we try simply does not work out—especially when "what you see year after year is misbehavior, disrespect, and middling improvement, and what you experience is stress and dissatisfaction, it's only natural to be a skeptic" (Linsin, 2021).

But there is hope. Linsin (2023) suggests a few things you can change to make your teaching life easier and improve classroom management:

- Working to set up your students for success by being clear on the rules and what is expected of them.
- Once again, avoid confrontation. This means not engaging with provocative behavior and the like. By doing this, they will see that you are not reactive to their challenges. You should work to be pleasant through all circumstances.

- Keep calm. There is no other way to say this. Avoid losing your patience and decide within yourself that, no matter what happens, you will not be taken to a place where you lack control.

- Write a classroom management plan where you establish the actions that need to be taken in case of misbehavior and challenging situations. This way, you will be prepared in case you need to face most situations by leaning on it.

- Make your students accountable. This means they should be responsible for what they are learning and for obtaining the best grades. You are there to teach them, but they should know they must be willing to participate and collaborate in order to achieve success.

- Tell them your expectations. You should be clear in verbalizing that you expect nothing less from them; that if you are giving your best, so should they; and that you want the highest quality of behavior and attitude they can deliver.

- Do not hold a grudge. If some days are better or worse even for us, the same can be said about students. They might not be on their best day, and if you are holding it against them, this might deteriorate a potentially positive relationship. Therefore, when you come into the class the next day, let go of what happened previously and start fresh.

Now that you have some tips on how to deal with your students, it is time that we talk about another common issue in the school environment: toxic colleagues. It is not everywhere that we will find only pleasant people to deal with, and just as certain individuals might rub us up the wrong way, others may feel the same about you. The key here is to always remain polite and not overstep in any situation. Let's take a look at some of the colleagues we may have to deal with and some ways to avoid having them taking away our peace.

Toxic colleagues

Sometimes it happens that managing a classroom is the *least* of your problems. Possibly because you have met at least one toxic colleague while in the school environment—it has happened to the best of us. They present themselves in many forms and manners, and usually they can make our brightest day seem cloudy and gray. If this has happened, or is happening, to you, let me say: you are not alone. I have been through it, and if you haven't, you are part of those in the "lucky" group.

These colleagues usually come in several types, from those who want to be on the administration's good side no matter what to those who always see the negative side of things. In addition to this, and worse, many of them have a toxic behavior toward not only other teachers but also their students. These include talking down to them, minimizing them for their test scores, and even escalating conflicts that did not necessarily need to be escalated.

Personally, I think one of the worst scenarios can be a colleague who insists on blaming a previous teacher for a student's poor performance. They will complain to the administration about the situation, acting as if the student or the circumstances played no part. Doesn't it sometimes feel like we are in the kindergarten playground all over again?

Not to mention those who seem to be spying on you to tell others what you are doing, the one who volunteers for everything and then complains about having too much to do, the other who always sees the negative side of things (also the contrary), and the one who is always positively toxic about everything. No matter what happens, we must learn how to deal with these individuals, no matter how much they bother us. I know it takes courage and patience to deal with these situations.

In these cases, the key is to essentially let go. I wouldn't advise confronting them, especially if the administration sees them in a good light. This could lead to a negative reflection on you. As you will see in the story at the end of this chapter in which I share my experience, this has happened to me. My course of action was to let it go and surpass the situation, hoping it would fade away. Eventually it did, but this took a lot of patience, resilience, and determination. Sometimes, we just need to focus on something else and understand that some people are just the way they are.

According to Barile (2020) and from my personal experience, here are a few things you should consider if you are faced with a toxic school environment:

- **Examine your attitude**: It could be the case that sometimes you *are* doing something that bothers the other person, but you are just not aware. Therefore, my recommendation is that the first thing you do is look at yourself and see if there are any points of self-improvement. If there are, you might want to speak to a union representative about courses you can take or learning opportunities that could be beneficial. I am not saying you are the problem, but sometimes a small change in our attitude might go a long way.

- **Work on self-care**: When we are stressed because of a toxic environment, it is likely we will go down a spiral that just never seems to end. When this is the case and you feel overwhelmed, take an evening to watch a movie, be with your loved ones, or do something you enjoy. This may lift up your spirit and make you feel better regarding the negative things going on in school. This will make you feel rejuvenated and able to come back to work the next day with a new determination and mood.

- **Talk to other people about it**: Sometimes, all we need to do is vent. However, it is important that you do this in a safe place and with people you can trust. I would advise against venting or speaking your heart out to another member of your school staff, for example: tides can change and you never know what will happen. If you feel the need to speak to another teacher, look for friends in other schools who might help you find a solution to your issue.

- **Stay positive**: No matter how bad things get, you must keep your head up and stay positive. Sometimes, we should recognize that the matter is not just with us but also with the other person. They might be dealing with some issues themselves and this is what makes them act this way. They might suffer from lack of confidence, need of affirmation, and many other issues. Remember to remain positive; this will help you see the situation with other eyes and get away from negativity.

- **Should I stay or should I go?**: One of our first reactions to a toxic environment is to say that we are going to give up, leave, and look for another job. If you feel this is the right thing for you, then you should. However, remember that all places have their challenges, and the ones you find in your next school could be different, for better or worse. The other option is to stay put and see how things develop. Sometimes, the problem will solve itself. You never know.

The last thing I want to say is that you should not feel bullied by these individuals. You should not let them take away your motivation to teach or to show up to school every day. It doesn't matter if they are constantly remarking that you are late or that they make snarky comments on how early you always are or how you stay late. Refuse to feel pushed around by these people. Don't be pushed away from doing what you love because of them. Remember that you are there for the students and for a purpose—even if sometimes you feel like you are not the right person to do the job. In other words, don't let imposter syndrome take you over.

Imposter syndrome

H ave you ever felt like a fraud, simply because you could not carry out the tasks you were hired to do? That you were so exhausted that you thought, *Am I doing the right thing? Is this where I am supposed to be?* If you have, then you are likely suffering from teacher imposter syndrome. Basically, this means that even though you have undergone the education and the training, you feel like you are not ready or prepared enough to undertake your current job.

Although this is not a feeling exclusive to teachers—it can affect professionals from all different industries—teachers usually feel like they are way out of their league, especially when dealing with a challenging classroom. They tend to question their abilities, their competence, their knowledge, and even if they are in the right place doing the right thing. This will, very possibly, impact your performance and the outcomes of how you manage a classroom and deal with the obstacles you are likely to face.

If you haven't experienced this feeling, then you are in the minority. As I mentioned earlier, most of us, lacking preparation to be effective in the classroom, feel this way when we are starting. I know I did. And since I did not have the support I needed from management, I was forced to find my own path and beat imposter syndrome on my own.

The first thing I did was look to other teachers for motivation. I used to see what they were doing and what worked for them. After this, I developed my own teaching personality, which meant I took all the things I observed that worked and added my own "spin" to it. Based on the situation I was experiencing or the challenge that presented itself, I developed my own approach to solving them. I started thinking differently. I understood that I had to look for success but also admit my failures so I could improve.

Finally, I adopted an "I can do it" mindset and reframed my thoughts to reflect that I was constantly learning and that there was no "right way" to do things. This significantly changed my vision on teaching and how I should act in the classroom. I learned that I should be not intimidated but rather inspired by carrying out change and making a difference. I learned to look at problems differently and find solutions rather than make them more overwhelming. I learned to be resilient.

A need for resilience

It is needless to say that difficulties in urban high schools are challenging. Sometimes, no matter how much material you prepare, how mentally tough you are, or how efficient your classroom management plan is, it just won't be enough. This drains us physically, but much more emotionally, since we never know when the next challenge might occur or when we will need to deal with a crisis. Because of this, it is essential that you be mentally prepared for what your students—or coworkers—will "throw" at you. For this specific reason, it is essential that, as educators, we develop resilience.

"Behavior management is often a tricky thing to master, especially at the early stages, but even very experienced teachers will be confronted with situations that they are not sure how best to respond to" (Ainsworth, n.d.). Although being more experienced means that you are likely to find solutions to these situations, it does not always mean that they won't be challenging. As a matter of fact, sometimes, because we are so set in our ways, we forget to think "outside the box" and find alternatives to student misbehavior. These attitudes can sometimes get the best of us and make us feel like the worst educators on the planet. To avoid this, learning to be resilient is an essential step to continue our development and learn how to keep control of problematic situations.

What is resilience for a teacher?

For some teachers, an act of misbehavior can ruin their day. It can be much worse if you keep it playing over and over in your mind and do not know how to bounce back from the situation. However, when we find emotional resilience, we are able to deal with the stress, or the trauma, in a way that we adapt our thoughts within our own mind to prevent it from causing further damage. But because we are teachers and we are dealing with younger individuals, these situations might be harder to overcome. It might be difficult to associate positive feelings with the student who is constantly disrupting class or the other who is continually challenging your authority.

For this reason, Ainsworth (n.d.) says that teacher resilience is a complex subject. According to the author, "Rather than considering resilience as a characteristic which sits inside an individual, it is more useful to think of resilience as a process which operates across the individual and their environment." This means that you must not only learn how to adapt your thoughts but think about the environment you are in and how it will all "fit" together. This also means that you must work on your emotional intelligence, self-confidence, and self-care since these are three of the characteristics that most successful professionals appear to have.

However, what is the prevalent feeling you have of the school? Is the administration supportive of your work? Do you have an exhaustive workload or do you consider it adequate? Are your colleagues positive or do they harbor a toxic environment? All of these questions should be taken into consideration when you think about the necessity to be resilient. Let's use an example to show you how it would work.

Suppose you find yourself with a student who is continually disrupting the class and challenging your authority. Maybe they are not pleasant and their interruptions prevent you from teaching the class. Not only do you need to have resilience within, but you should be sure that the environment favors you as well. If you were to punish this student, would the school administration back you up? Would they be supportive of the actions you take to ensure that you have the class under control? If the answer is no, they would just dismiss it, then you will become frustrated, no matter how much you practice and apply resilience.

All these questions should be asked to help you improve your resilient characteristics. There is no need to mention that when the environment isn't favorable, we won't feel that the effort is worth it. If you feel overwhelmed with work, you might think, *this is just not worth it, why should I bother?* and move on to teach as best you can. As you can see, your work conditions have a deep impact on how you "bounce back" from problems and challenges.

Mallon (2022) mentions a few techniques that can be used to improve your resilience:

- Having a social life where you can decompress and share your anxiety with your friends or loved ones. They will be your support in being more resilient when difficult situations appear and you feel like there is no way out.

- Working on emotional intelligence, which essentially means that you will not let your emotions get the best of you in these situations. You should work to be aware of your emotions and how they make you react when there is a problem so you can identify them when they show up—either in yourself or in others.

- Developing a mindset where you will establish your purpose, your values, and the things that matter to you. You will also work on thinking that you can do it, you are able to do it, and you do have the skills and necessary tools to deal with the issue.

- Job crafting, by which you will take control of the situation and be proactive when the problem appears. As you will see, the Stoics said that you should worry only about the things that you can control and let go of the things you cannot. When adopting this in your life, you will see that you will feel more empowered and positive when dealing with challenges.

- Caring for yourself, because if you do not, no one else will! This means taking the weekend off to do something you love with the family, it means having time to exercise and take care of your well-being, and having enough time to rest for the next day. You should also consider taking breaks throughout the day, just to have five minutes to yourself.

Essentially, it is important that, as an educator and an individual, you know what your values are and that you are guided by them. When we feel like we are following what we believe in, we find it easier to be resilient. Think about the times when you had to go against what you thought was right. How did that make you feel? Possibly not the best, and this does nothing to help you build up resilience. Therefore, you should constantly focus on what is important to you and how you are going to apply and show this in your classroom. You know what matters, and this is what is important. When you have this clear, it will be clear to others as well.

Next, you must be able to reflect on your actions and assure yourself that you did the right thing. This means you are going to think about the actions you took and see if it was the right path, if you would have done anything different, or even if you let your emotions get involved in the situation. It is likely that most of the time, there will be things we could change or do differently. However, you must make this a learning experience and evaluate what happened. Once you are able to reflect on these circumstances, you will be in an ongoing learning process that will only enrich your knowledge and make you more resilient and a better educator.

Finally, when we have a clear view of what we believe in and how we feel about certain situations, it is possible to establish boundaries regarding things we can and cannot accept. This means "pulling the plug" on situations that make you uncomfortable or that are even dangerous: acting on what you believe is correct. There must be a limit to the things that you are willing to tolerate or overlook and those that you are going to take action upon. Most importantly, as Aguilar (2022) said, when we establish boundaries, we are saving our energy by not letting students, our coworkers, or the administration dictate what we should and should not be doing.

The case of Mr. X

I was a dedicated teacher, passionate about my subject, and committed to helping my students succeed. But the principal of my school, let's call him Mr. X, had a personal vendetta against me. Whenever he observed my classes, he found a way to give me a negative evaluation. According to his reports, everything I did was ineffective. It didn't matter that I had students working in groups, going to the blackboard, and completing charts and Venn diagrams to support my lessons. It was demoralizing and frustrating to receive such unjust criticism.

During post-observation meetings, the principal would tell me that I was not meeting expectations and that I would be fired from the New York City Department of Education by September 2015. But I refused to let his toxic behavior defeat me. I tried to find ways to improve my teaching and demonstrate my competence, but nothing I did could please him. Drawing on the principles of Stoic philosophy, I remained patient and resilient in the face of adversity.

Then, one day, the toxic principal emailed the entire staff, announcing that a new principal would take over his position the next day. Reading this, I felt relieved and decided to respond to the email. I quoted Lord Buddha: "Whatever you do, you do it to yourself." I wished the outgoing principal luck and moved on to a new chapter in my teaching career.

* * *

Mr. X had been removed from his position as principal because several corruption charges had led the New York City Department of Education to pay millions of dollars in lawsuits. Mr. X managed to become a Dean at another school; I knew he would never be able to do the same damage he did to me and other teachers at my old school. I was proud of myself for standing up to him and not letting him get the best of me.

A few years later, the Department of Education closed that school for poor performance, and I became an ATR (Attendance Teacher Resource). An ATR is a teacher who does not have a permanent assignment at a school. Therefore, the ATR supports different schools until they find one that finally hires them permanently. I remember one day, walking through the halls of a school where I was assigned as an ATR, I saw someone I recognized: Mr. X, the former school principal who had unfairly given me negative evaluations during class observations. There he was, now working as a Dean at this school. I couldn't believe my eyes.

Despite how he had treated me in the past, I decided to keep quiet about our history. I didn't want to create any problems, and I didn't want to gossip or make anyone feel uncomfortable. So I just smiled at him as we passed each other in the hallway.

Knowing what he had put me through, I felt strange seeing him again. But I also felt a sense of satisfaction. I was resilient and patient in the face of his unfair evaluations and predictions that I would be fired. And now, here I am, still teaching and making a difference in students' lives.

As you might have noticed, I used the words "Stoic philosophy" and "Stoicism" a couple times in the chapter. This is because I have found their teachings to be not just theoretical but also highly practical for high school teachers. Based on this philosophy, I have gained a clearer understanding of when I should act and take control, empowering me in my role as an educator.

Undoubtedly, the timeless wisdom of Stoicism has emerged as an invaluable companion in the daily challenges and struggles of educators. Its principles have not just guided but also inspired me toward personal growth, resilience, and the discernment to act purposefully within our sphere of influence. I believe it can do the same for you.

With this in mind, I warmly invite you to join me in the next chapter. Together, we will explore how awareness can assist us in resolving school-related conflicts. Your unique perspectives and experiences are invaluable in this shared journey.

As we embark on the next exploration phase, we will delve into the transformative power of awareness, a cornerstone of the Stoic philosophy. By cultivating present-moment awareness, we will uncover the secrets to navigating conflicts and challenges with clarity, wisdom, and equanimity.

Bibliography

Aguilar, E. (2022). The resilient educator/What does a resilient educator do? *ASCD*. Retrieved from https://www.ascd.org/el/articles/the-resilient-educator-what-does-a-resilient-educator-do

Ainsworth, S. (n.d.). What is resilience for a teacher? *FutureLearn*. Retrieved from https://www.futurelearn.com/info/courses/succeed-as-a-new-teacher/0/steps/147289

Ashleigh. (2019, September 1). 5 reasons for student misbehavior. *Ashleigh's Education Journey*. Retrieved from https://www.ashleigh-educationjourney.com/5-reasons-for-student-misbehavior/

Banks, A. (2020, April 22). Why do children misbehave? Finding the root causes of classroom misbehavior. *Insights to Behavior*. Retrieved from https://insightstobehavior.com/blog/children-misbehave-finding-root-classroom-misbehavior

Barile, N. (2020, February 18). Surviving a toxic school environment. *Hey Teach!* Retrieved from https://www.wgu.edu/heyteach/article/surviving-a-toxic-school-environment2002.html

Daily Stoic. (n.d.). How to develop stoic mental toughness and resilience. Retrieved from https://dailystoic.com/seth-haselhuhn

Linsin, M. (2021, April 3). Why so many teachers struggle with classroom management. *Smart Classroom Management*. Retrieved from https://smartclassroommanagement.com/2021/04/03/teachers-struggle-with-classroom-management

Linsin, M. (2023, January 7). 7 small, simple classroom management resolutions for 2023. *Smart Classroom Management*. Retrieved from https://smartclassroommanagement.com/2023/01/06/classroom-management-resolutions-2023

Mallon, R. (2022). Why is teacher resilience important? *Twinkl*. Retrieved from https://www.twinkl.com.ph/blog/why-is-teacher-resilience-important

CHAPTER 5

The Power of Awareness

Embracing Stoic Mindfulness

DOI: 10.4324/9781003535652-6

66 Life is very short and anxious for those who forget the past, neglect the present, and fear the future.

Seneca, *On the Shortness of Life*

It is likely you have heard the word "mindfulness" sometime during your life. Mindfulness is about being present and aware of what is going around us—essentially to be present in the present (Staff, 2020). This has been a pretty big concept. It has changed the lives of many people who were too concerned over past actions, and it has helped decrease their anxiety when thinking about the future. This can include activities such as walking, meditating, and making a conscious observation of what is around you.

The practice helps many people daily, and there is even a proven psychological effect to putting it into operation (National Institutes of Health, 2021). The most important part is learning how to be aware of yourself and your behavior. While this might seem like something a Stoic would do, there are some differences between Stoic mindfulness and mindfulness as it is seen more commonly. In this chapter, we are going to explore the nuances of the Stoic approach and, more importantly, how you can apply it to your life. If you are already familiar with the concept and have been applying it, you will see that all it takes is a different approach to modify the direction of your actions. Shall we take a look?

The philosophy of Stoic mindfulness

When we consider mindfulness, we understand it as being present and aware of our experiences. The Stoic principle aligns with this notion but has a significant distinction: our attention is directed solely toward what is within our control (Ussher, 2013). While traditional mindfulness encourages paying attention to all aspects of the present moment, Stoics emphasize directing our energy and actions toward things we can actively change. To gain a deeper understanding, we can ask ourselves: am I focusing on the present moment while focusing on something within my control? This shift in perspective allows us to harness our efforts and prioritize our attention toward what truly matters.

Suppose you are in the teachers' lounge, overhearing two colleagues discussing the difficulty of obtaining support from the Department of Education to pay overtime to help struggling students. While being mindful and aware of the situation, you realize that the Department of Education's actions and budget are beyond your control. Consequently, you cannot propose any solution that relies on their involvement. Recognizing these limitations and shifting your focus to actionable steps within your sphere of influence are crucial. By accepting what you cannot control, you can channel your energy toward finding alternative solutions that address the needs of your students effectively.

Imagine this: you stumble upon a neighboring school's program that offers student tutoring in exchange for spending time with elders at a care facility. It may not be groundbreaking, but it provides companionship and entertainment for older people. The crucial point is that you can propose this solution to the school administration or the teachers involved. Rather than emphasizing a sense of helplessness, you actively engage by suggesting a concrete action. By presenting viable alternatives, you foster empowerment and initiate positive change.

As a Stoic educator, you focus on finding solutions rather than dwelling on negativity or proposing potentially rejected ideas. Considering the possible benefits for both students and the situation, suggesting extra tutoring classes becomes a win-win scenario, pending approval from the school administration. Taking matters into your own hands, you advocate for this solution, acknowledging that your role is to support rather than make the final decision. Ultimately, the responsibility rests with those in authority to determine the course of action. By embracing this mindset, you empower yourself to contribute positively within the boundaries of your influence.

Can you see the difference in approach? "In short, a basic Stoic mindfulness practice might be to ask yourself at different points throughout the day: 'Where am I placing myself in this situation?'" (Ussher, 2013). In the situation above, the issue was directly related to you, since it would benefit your students. However, the approach can be controversial, because you will only be inserted in situations directly affecting you and making a difference in your life, even though you can help control it for the sake of others.

Some people might say that this is a "selfish" approach, but this is because of the lack of a greater understanding of the philosophy. If you remember what you have read before, Stoics are all about sharing wisdom and being altruistic, compassionate, and empathic to other people's situations. Therefore, if you are going to act for the "good," you can most certainly interfere and cooperate with others if you feel that your involvement will bring a positive outcome to the situation.

> Stoic mindfulness is really about seeing what is up to you in any given situation, focussing [sic] on doing that well and on doing the act with kindness towards others. It is from the Stoics, indeed, that the ideal of a 'community of humankind' first stems.
>
> (Ussher, 2013)

Embracing Stoic philosophy as an educator means aligning your actions with your values and beliefs and seeking positive outcomes. Remember the principle of *amor fati*, accepting things as they are intended to be. Adopting a broader perspective allows you to analyze situations, distinguishing what you can influence from what is beyond your control. Shift your focus to what you can change and make decisions based on wisdom, courage, justice, and temperance. Prioritize the well-being of the collective over personal ego. Though you may feel limited in influencing broader policies or others' attitudes, remember that your impact extends beyond external factors.

Direct your efforts toward what is within your reach—nurturing student growth and fostering positive relationships within the school community. Stoic mindfulness becomes a powerful tool for navigating challenges and cultivating resilience. Embodying Stoic principles creates a positive learning environment, empowering individuals to thrive.

Unlock your potential as an educator by embracing Stoic principles and adopting a holistic perspective. While you can't control every aspect of the educational environment, you can shape students' experiences and those directly connected to you. Embrace the power of Stoicism to cultivate resilience, inspire growth, and foster positive change within yourself and your educational community.

Ways mindfulness can help teachers

As a dedicated educator, you may wonder why you should add mindfulness to your busy schedule, filled with lesson planning, managing challenging students, and navigating a demanding school environment. I understand your concerns. But what if I told you that adopting mindful techniques could help you manage your classroom more effectively and reduce the stress you experience? Imagine the impact that would have on your job satisfaction. So, let's approach mindfulness differently, considering how it can benefit you.

Research suggests that mindfulness in the classroom can lead to reduced conflict and student–teacher relationships that are more positive, ultimately enhancing overall job satisfaction (Jennings, 2015). The mere thought of experiencing less stress during demanding lessons is undoubtedly appealing. And the best part is that you can unlock these advantages by making minor changes to your daily routine.

Take a moment to reflect on your reactions to classroom situations. Are your responses impulsive, driven by knee-jerk reactions? Or do you pause, take a deep breath, and consider your next steps? When faced with disruptive behavior, we often scold students and quickly lose patience. But what if I told you their intention is to provoke you? Maintaining your composure and responding consciously can make your actions less effective.

Consider the challenging students you encounter in your classes. It's common to approach them with preconceived notions, expecting the worst. However, this mindset can lead to losing patience and disrupting the entire class. You can change the dynamics by shifting to a different approach, one that involves conscious communication and a genuine understanding of their feelings and motivations. Imagine the impact it could have on their behavior and the overall classroom atmosphere.

Embracing mindfulness as a teacher may seem like an additional responsibility, but it offers transformative benefits. Incorporating mindful practices into your daily routine can enhance your ability to manage challenges, create a positive classroom environment, and foster stronger connections with your students. The power to improve your teaching experience, and the lives of your students, lies in making intentional shifts in your mindset and approach.

Sometimes, it is as simple as pausing and analyzing the situation to find a positive way forward. For instance, instead of reacting to a disruptive student, you can choose not to engage, eventually discouraging their disruptive behavior. Alternatively, you may discover that a need for attention drives their behavior. In that case, giving them focused attention can make a difference. "Giving each student our full mindful attention for even a short period of class time gives them the message 'I see you.' By connecting with our students, we let them know we value them as individuals" (Jennings, 2015).

Let us do a small exercise together to illustrate this point. Are you willing to give it a try? Think about the most recent incident with a disobedient student in your class. How did you react? Take a moment to reflect: what were you thinking about at that moment? Were you fully present in the class or preoccupied with other thoughts? In other words, were you truly engaged in the present moment and aware of your surroundings? Your answer may be "no." If that is the case, let us shift our thinking and consider: If you were fully present in the classroom, attentively observing your students and your feelings, would your reaction have been the same? Would you have been better able to control the impulse to react? Would you have been better able to understand the underlying need? Were external conditions and internal thoughts controlling you, or were you controlling them?

With almost 100% certainty, you might have been preoccupied with something else or another issue or concern in that situation. You were likely not fully present in the classroom. Your reaction was influenced by letting your emotions dictate your actions. Ultimately, this means you were not approaching your lesson or students with mindfulness, which they sensed, and as a result you lost your temper.

However, I understand that simply pointing out these issues without offering solutions is not helpful. As the Stoics say, we also need to teach and share our wisdom, which is precisely what I intend to do now. I want to provide you with practical tools that have worked for me and, perhaps, will enable you to effortlessly adopt a mindful approach to your classes. By doing so, you will experience a decrease in stress and dissatisfaction. I aim to guide you toward finding inner peace, which will support you as a Stoic educator.

Finding inner peace

One of the most essential tools to finding the inner peace you desire is practicing self-control. You can make a significant difference in your life by managing your emotions, attitudes, and reactions. Part of self-control is accepting the things you cannot change and asking yourself, *Is it worth stressing over?* If the situation is beyond your control, remember to accept fate as it is and practice *amor fati*. Epictetus wisely said, "Do not seek things to happen the way you want them to; instead, wish for things to happen the way they happen, and you will find happiness" (Wise Towl, 2020).

Another essential aspect is self-analysis, which allows you to find inner peace. Take a moment to step back and imagine viewing the situation from above as a third person, detached from the emotions involved. How are you reacting? Are you giving too much importance to trivial matters? Remember that sometimes, not reacting is the best course of action. You do not have to let everything affect you. By adopting an attitude of indifference toward things that do not matter, you shield yourself from unnecessary pain and turmoil (Wise Towl, 2020).

Stoic negative visualization is a powerful technique to prepare for life's challenges, including those encountered in the classroom. By envisioning and considering the worst-case scenarios, you can proactively plan and develop strategies to overcome obstacles. While we hope for positive and fruitful days at school, visualizing potential adversity helps us respond positively rather than impulsively, based on emotions.

Self-reflection and journaling are practices embraced by some Stoics to gain insight into their thoughts, actions, and emotions. Writing down your experiences gives you a clearer perspective on what transpired. Marcus Aurelius, known for his *Meditations*, wrote extensively in his journal. When journaling, focus on events and the lessons learned and wisdom gained from teachers, readings, and personal experiences (Wise Towl, 2020).

Finally, ask yourself this vital question: If today were your last day, would you feel content and proud of your actions? Are you practicing *memento mori*, the contemplation of mortality? Are you making the most of the situations you encounter? If you can confidently answer yes, rest assured that you are applying the four Stoic virtues to the classroom. However, if you have any doubts or areas for improvement, seize the opportunity to put them into practice. Leading a fulfilling life means guiding your students toward knowledge, education, and self-awareness, molding them into better individuals for the future. Embrace this journey and strive to make a positive impact within your classroom.

Using mindfulness as a tool

I have faced various challenges as a teacher, including difficult students and toxic colleagues. However, Stoic mindfulness has proven effective, even when dealing with a challenging school administrator.

Once, I encountered a mean and relentless administrator who seemed determined to make my life unbearable. They constantly criticized my teaching methods and questioned my abilities. Imagine: this person did not even speak another language and wanted to indoctrinate me on how I would teach a language to my students (before becoming an Assistant Principal or AP, they were a Math teacher; Math was their specialty). Instead of allowing their maltreatment to affect me, I chose to apply Stoic mindfulness.

By remaining composed and not engaging with their negativity, I found that something remarkable happened. The administrator gradually grew tired of their futile attempts to provoke a reaction. Eventually, they accepted a position at another school, and the following year, they were no longer at our institution.

Being extroverted, I have always found it challenging to remain calm in the face of injustice and disrespect, as my natural tendency is to speak up and confront mean-spirited individuals. However, Stoic mindfulness has proven to be a powerful reminder of how mindfulness can create positive shifts and seemingly work miracles. By staying present and mindful, I have maintained my integrity as an educator and positively influenced the dynamics within public schools.

Stoic mindfulness empowers me to rise above challenges, fostering a more harmonious environment for myself and my students. Do I ever doubt myself? Do I speak up? Absolutely! It's not about suppressing who you are. Someone once told me, "God dwells in you as you." However, after embracing Stoic practices, I choose my battles wisely.

The practice of Stoic mindfulness has been transformative. It has enabled me to cultivate heightened awareness and presence in adversity. It has empowered me to respond to challenges with wisdom and equanimity, creating a more harmonious and conducive environment for learning and growth.

Embracing mindfulness does not mean suppressing one's authentic self. Instead, it provides the discernment to choose battles wisely, focus energy on what truly matters, and let go of what is beyond our control.

Stoic mindfulness has guided me in navigating adversity and nurturing resilience, allowing me to embody Stoic principles and create a transformative educational experience.

The synergy between Stoic philosophy and mindfulness is a potent catalyst for personal growth and professional excellence. By embodying these teachings, I have cultivated a deep resilience, enabling me to navigate the educational landscape's challenges with grace and wisdom.

While the power of Stoic mindfulness has been a profound source of strength and resilience, the journey of personal growth and self-mastery extends beyond individual practice. In the next chapter, we will explore the vital role that healthy relationships play in creating a nurturing and supportive educational environment.

Positive relationships are the bedrock of a thriving educational community. They foster a sense of belonging, trust, and mutual respect, creating an atmosphere conducive to learning, growth, and personal development.

We will uncover the secrets to effective communication, conflict resolution, and cultivating empathy and understanding through practical strategies and real-life examples. We will also explore the importance of setting boundaries while maintaining an open and inclusive approach, fostering an environment where diverse perspectives are valued and celebrated.

Prepare to embark on a journey of self-discovery and interpersonal growth, where the principles of Stoicism and mindfulness will serve as a foundation for building meaningful connections and creating a transformative educational experience for all involved.

Bibliography

Jennings, P. (2015, March 30). Seven ways mindfulness can help teachers. *Greater Good*. Retrieved from https://greatergood.berkeley.edu/article/item/seven_ways_mindfulness_can_help_teachers

National Institutes of Health. (2021, June 1). Mindfulness for your health. *News in Health*. Retrieved from https://newsinhealth.nih.gov/2021/06/mindfulness-your-health

Staff, M. (2020, July 8). What is mindfulness? *Mindful*. Retrieved from https://www.mindful.org/what-is-mindfulness

Ussher, P. (2013, November 28). The philosophy of Stoic mindfulness. *Modern Stoicism*. Retrieved from https://modernstoicism.com/features-the-philosophy-of-stoic-mindfulness-by-patrick-ussher

Wise Towl. (2020, March 10). 7 Stoic exercises for inner peace. *TOWL*. Retrieved from https://www.towl.us/blogs/mindful-owl-journal/7-stoic-exercises-for-inner-peace

CHAPTER 6
Cultivating Positive Relationships

DOI: 10.4324/9781003535652-7

> If you really want to escape the things that harass you, what you're needing is not to be in a different place but to be a different person.

Seneca, *Letters from a Stoic*

Part of my job as a teacher has been to aid students in resolving conflict, especially between peers. However, you probably know that it is not only with students that we must navigate these issues. Conflict is a daily part of our jobs. Whether you are struggling with finding the appropriate budget to carry out the activities we have planned (there is almost always not enough), making sure our students are receiving adequate academic support (most need extra tutoring classes they do not have access to), or with parents who are aggressive and not participating in their child's education (I bet you have met quite a few of these), you have certainly been required to deal with conflict in the school environment—without mentioning struggles with other teachers, administration, and so on.

While your first instinct when you see that individual with "steam coming out of their heads" approaching you is to run, sometimes it is important to participate and engage in conflict. This is because conflict, "when it's healthy, productive, and progress-focused, can be an amazing tool in your toolbox, whether you're dealing with it in your personal life, or with your colleagues and within your team" (Yackowski, 2021). However, in order to effectively and productively use this tool to build positive relationships, it is important that you know what to do. Therefore, in this chapter, we will explore the Stoic approach to conflict management and how you can apply its teachings in your class, with your students, with other teachers, and even in dealing with all the other agents involved in your daily school routine.

Conflict management

If you ever witness or find yourself in a conflict, your initial instinct will likely be to jump to conclusions. Whether based on your observations or the words of others involved, our perception of the situation often shapes our judgments and evaluations. However, what if I told you that even amid conflict, the best approach is to adopt a broader perspective? While it may be easier to maintain objectivity from the outside, it becomes significantly more challenging when you are unwillingly entangled in the issue.

Epictetus offers valuable insight on handling conflict: "Do not let the force of an impression carry you away. Say to it, 'Hold up a bit and let me see who you are and where you are from—let me put you to the test'" (Yackowski, 2021). This is easier said than done, especially when dealing with individuals who wear their emotions on their sleeves or refuse to engage in rational discussion. In such instances, our instinct is to become defensive and allow our emotions to take control. However, as a Stoic educator, you will understand this is not the appropriate response.

It is crucial to step back and view the situation from an external perspective or, at the very least, the other person's perspective. As the saying goes, "There are two sides to every coin." Just as you have your interpretation of a particular issue, the other person will have theirs, and the two may not align. This disparity in viewpoints often leads to conflicts in the first place. To arrive at an optimal solution, it is vital to consider the perspective you are adopting. You may see only a fragment of the more significant problem and need help to grasp the whole picture.

This is where Stoic values come into play. Employing wisdom, courage, temperance, and justice, you can understand situations reasonably and make well-informed assessments that lead to the best decisions.

Sometimes, if it is beyond your control, the best course of action is to let go. However, to determine the appropriate course, the first step is to gather all relevant information that has led to the conflict.

In doing so, you are employing the Stoic value of wisdom. Wisdom entails gathering information, practicing patience, and actively listening. Hearing all parties involved will give you a deeper understanding of the situation and offer valuable insights for resolving the matter. It will also equip you with the necessary information to make a fair decision, ensuring justice for all parties involved.

However, to accomplish this, we must confront the fear and other emotions that overwhelm us during conflicts. Courage may be required to speak up and assert yourself or to stand up for what you believe is right. Conflict can trigger intense positive and negative emotions, and this is where your Stoic understanding becomes crucial. Do not allow your emotions to cloud your judgment or undermine your ability to exercise self-control. Regardless of the complexity of the matter, it is essential that you, as the mediator, remain calm, acknowledge your feelings, and strive for the best possible outcome for all parties involved.

Approaching conflict management from a Stoic perspective is more than "winning" the conflict. It is about reaching the most favorable decision for all parties. While the other party may not share your approach to resolving conflicts, you will find that it ultimately brings you benefits. Like other Stoic practices, the more you exercise and embrace this approach, the more proficient you will become. While adjusting to this new mindset may take time initially, you will soon discover that it often leads to positive outcomes.

Benefits of Stoicism in the workplace

To understand the benefits of adopting a Stoic approach to conflict, let us consider the words of Marcus Aurelius, the Roman emperor, who frequently dealt with conflict resolution. He advised us to start each day by acknowledging that the people we interact with may be meddling, ungrateful, arrogant, dishonest, jealous, and surly (Bonnie, 2017). While this may seem harsh, people are often driven by self-interest and not concerned with fairness or balanced decisions. Our task becomes more challenging when we encounter such individuals, especially those driven by ego rather than character and virtue.

This is when our Stoic toolkit comes into play. By employing rationality, a characteristic often lacking in others, we can analyze the situation and understand what is truly happening. We may realize that the person seeks the most straightforward way out, preferring to remove a disruptive student from class rather than address the underlying issues. Alternatively, we could observe someone expressing their emotions without restraint, such as a parent blaming us for their child's poor academic performance, without considering their role in the child's lack of attention.

Approaching the situation with perspective, calmness, and rationality allows us to see it more clearly and provide a better assessment. By aligning our thoughts and desires with what is morally right and honest, we remain true to our values. This approach makes conflict management easier and enables us to address the heated reactions of others more effectively.

It is essential to remember that we must first be true to ourselves because we have to live with the decisions we make. As Marcus Aurelius noted, we tend to care more about others' opinions than our own, but we should prioritize our judgment (Bonnie, 2017). Maintaining calmness and emotional control grants us greater rationality and strength to proceed.

We understand that it is not easy. We may feel the urge to react when someone criticizes our teaching or undermines our abilities or when the support staff fails to assist us or the administration blames us for a student's disruptive behavior. It is unfair when judgment is passed without full knowledge of the situation.

However, resilience is vital. Through practicing negative visualization, we prepare ourselves for adversity, knowing what to expect and considering the worst possible outcome. We can then ask ourselves: How can we handle this challenge to bring fairness and satisfaction to all parties involved? What aspects of the situation can we control? How can we resolve the conflict in the best interest of the student, parent, administration, and ourselves? Ultimately, we are there to teach and guide our students, and by managing unpredictable situations assertively and rationally, we find that our chances of success improve.

Acknowledging that everyone has their values is essential, and finding common ground can be difficult. Sometimes, the best course of action is to accept the situation and explore alternative options. It is common to encounter individuals who resist change and refuse to accept mutually beneficial outcomes. For example, toxic behavior from school administrations may lead to blaming teachers rather than addressing their ineffectiveness. However, there are strategies to deal with such challenging individuals, which we will discuss later.

By embracing a Stoic approach to conflict management, we aim not merely to "win" the conflict but to reach the best decision for all parties involved. While others may have different approaches, we can appreciate personal growth and positive outcomes that stem from applying Stoic principles. With practice, we become better at managing conflicts and realize that our rationality and adherence to Stoic values contribute to successful resolutions.

Dealing with difficult people

We have all encountered these:

- the colleagues who fuss about every little thing
- the demanding superiors who are never satisfied
- the passive-aggressive individuals who smile while launching subtle attacks

As educators, we come across toxic people—entitled, greedy, lazy, or control freaks—who seem to drain our energy. However, fear not, for Stoic philosophy offers valuable insights on how to navigate such encounters.

By now, you understand the importance of being prepared. Practicing negative visualization equips you with a mental shield to face the challenges of each day. However, there are times when preparation alone falls short. Despite our efforts to rise above and control our emotions, specific individuals have a knack for getting under our skin, leaving us powerless and unable to reason.

In such moments, take a deep breath. Pause, examine your emotions, but remember not to let them overpower you. Be honest with yourself about your feelings but refrain from displaying them outwardly. People do not need to know. Instead, shift your focus to the other person. Truly observe them. Understand that they are also individuals shaped by their unique experiences, backgrounds, and perspectives. They might lack the tools to manage their emotions, or they might struggle to control their thoughts and actions.

Approach the other person empathetically and alter your perception of them. As Willis (2020) astutely notes, our natural tendency is to scrutinize the faults of others after unpleasant interactions, ruminating over what we would have done differently or cataloging their transgressions. Can you recall a recent instance when you stopped dwelling on their shortcomings and instead contemplated how your actions could change the situation?

Maintaining rationality during challenging encounters can be demanding. Sometimes, you wish to escape a staff meeting and find solace in a place where your contributions are valued, where productivity and efficiency reign. Instead you are listening to complaints and witnessing dysfunctional processes. However, if you have already visualized these adverse reactions, you have likely considered potential solutions to the issues at hand. While you cannot control how the other person will respond to your Stoic approach, remaining steadfast in your values and being guided by wisdom, fairness, and integrity increase the likelihood of a positive outcome.

Difficult or toxic individuals often do not expect such behavior from others. Consumed by their thoughts and actions, they fail to consider their negative impact on those around them. Nevertheless, we should remember that it is our "job" to change not them but rather ourselves—our perspective on the world and the situations we find ourselves in. When you shift your focus from the flaws of others to your growth, true transformation unfolds. Once again, the words of Marcus Aurelius resonate: "It is futile to escape the faults of others; they are inevitable. Instead, focus on escaping your own" (Willis, 2020). In other words, embrace the Stoic maxim of accepting what is beyond your control.

Is it challenging? Undoubtedly. Does it require practice? Absolutely. However, as you master the art of handling such situations, you will discover a newfound strength within you—a superpower. When we learn to manage these encounters and realize that change must begin with us rather than expecting others to change, our perspective on challenging relationships undergoes a profound shift. Sometimes, taking action means refraining from engaging, allowing people consumed by their thoughts and emotions to exist without our interference. In some instances, simply letting them be is the wisest choice.

Applying Stoicism to challenging situations

I was a young teacher starting at a challenging public school in the Bronx, NY. Mrs. Domina, a harsh foreign language Assistant Principal, notorious for being difficult with teachers and students, came to observe one of my Spanish classes. During the lesson, she suddenly interrupted me, shouting that it wasn't working and demanding to see a "real lesson." She summoned me to her office the next day, and I spent a sleepless night imagining the worst.

In my desperation, I turned to a maxim by Seneca: "If you want to escape the things that harass you, what you need is not to be in a different place but to be a different person" (Seneca, n.d.). Inspired by this, I decided to arrive at her office as a mature professional who deserved respect, not as a young teacher needing advice.

As soon as I arrived at the meeting, I stunned Mrs. Domina by asking her to sign my "pink slip" so I could leave the school immediately. (In the late 1990s and early 2000s, the pink slip in the New York City Department of Education used to be an Employment Release Form that principals and APs would sign to release teachers from a public school.) I gave her a blank pink slip to sign. When she asked why, I explained that I had felt disrespected and humiliated in front of my students the day before and didn't feel valued or appreciated. Mrs. Domina seemed taken aback and tried to convince me to stay. She apologized for her impulsive outburst and acknowledged that she was concerned about my talent as a young teacher.

During the meeting, Mrs. Domina not only offered me valuable tips on improving my classroom management but also acknowledged my service as a teacher. This interaction marked the beginning of a professional relationship built on mutual respect. Despite the negative opinions some colleagues held about her, I discovered that approaching challenging situations with confidence and professionalism could lead to unexpected growth, a growth that I am sure each of you can also achieve.

This anecdote is a powerful testament to the transformative impact of cultivating positive relationships. A once-strained dynamic was transformed into a foundation of mutual respect and growth by approaching the situation with confidence, professionalism, and an open mind.

While some chose to dwell in negativity, I found that embracing a positive and constructive approach opened doors to unforeseen opportunities and personal development, a testament to the potential for growth and change that lies within each of us. This experience underscores the significance of fostering healthy relationships, not just with students but also with colleagues, administrators, and the broader educational community.

As we reflect on the profound insights and practical strategies explored throughout this journey, it becomes evident that the principles of Stoicism hold immense potential for transforming the educational landscape. In the upcoming chapter, "The Stoic Educator: Transforming Lives Through Stoic Principles," we will synthesize the wisdom and teachings we have acquired, crafting a comprehensive vision that enlightens us on what it truly means to be a Stoic educator.

This chapter will guide us in applying the threads of resilience, mindfulness, positive relationships, and mastery of our sphere of influence in the classroom. We will explore the core tenets of Stoic philosophy and their practical applications, demonstrating how these timeless principles can shape our approach to teaching, managing the classroom, and cultivating a nurturing learning environment.

Bibliography

Bonnie, E. (2017, May 1). Stop playing nice! The Stoic's guide to managing workplace conflict. *Wrike*. Retrieved from https://www.wrike.com/blog/stoics-guide-managing-workplace-conflict/#Conflict-is-Inevitable

Seneca. (n.d.). If you really want to escape the things that harass you, what you're needing is not to be in a different place but to be a different person. *Goodreads*. Retrieved from https://www.goodreads.com/quotes/881646-if-you-really-want-to-escape-the-things-that-harass

Willis, A. (2020, April 11). Stoic principles for dealing with difficult people. *Medium; The Apeiron Blog*. Retrieved from https://theapeiron.co.uk/stoic-principles-for-dealing-with-difficult-people-20c2cd399fad

Yackowski, A. (2021, March 16). *A Stoic Approach to Conflict*. LinkedIn. https://www.linkedin.com/pulse/power-perspective-amy-yackowski/

CHAPTER 7

The Stoic Educator

Transforming Lives Through Stoic Principles

DOI: 10.4324/9781003535652-8

> 66 It's not what happens to you but how you react to it that matters.

Epictetus, *Enchiridion*

I hope that by now you are able to understand, as the quote that you see at the beginning of the chapter says, that the key to being a Stoic educator, to see things change, is to carry out the change within yourself. Harding (2015) says that high school students today are too absorbed in their mobile phones, celebrity culture, and other superfluous issues that take them away from knowing their real abilities and understanding that their parents love them. Because of this, he divides the group into two: those who are narcissistic and those who are neurotic.

In this situation, Harding (2015) says, "The narcissists believe they are very important; the neurotics believe they are perpetually under threat." Can you identify with this situation in your classroom? In either case, the teacher will have a natural response to these behaviors, which is to act with anger toward the narcissist and with exasperation toward the neurotic. Nevertheless, the Stoic teacher will understand that they cannot change either of these conditions, and it is essential that they learn how to deal with them and change their own behavior toward the matter. In this instance, the teacher can try acting, where they "can choose to demonstrate courage and resolve to the narcissist and understanding and compassion to the neurotic, and through his behavior show that an alternative is possible, while realizing that it will likely matter to no-one [sic]."

It can also be useless to complain to the school administration. The principal and superintendent sometimes don't seem to care or are too busy with political matters to deal with "normal" classroom issues. Other teachers are too busy dealing with their own problems to help you out, apart from some specific cases. It thus relies on us, the teachers, to take the matter into our own hands and solve the problem with the best alternatives we can think of. Thinking of this, I developed a pedagogical method that focuses on the student and making them see the positive things they can experience in school—the Marvel Education method.

Together with the Stoic approach to a teacher's behavior regarding their environment and the situations they face, they must also work to "enchant" the student and direct them toward the right path. Although you can learn more about this approach in the book of the same name, I want to bring you some of the highlights and show you how it can be associated with Stoic philosophy to provide you with a better teaching environment. Under this circumstance, you will find that you have a more cooperative class, fewer student behavior problems, and an easier time navigating your daily school life.

The beauty of questions

When you feel the need to engage the class, one of the best ways to do this is to motivate them to ask questions. Teachers should think outside the box and question their students about their views, opinions, and thoughts. Likewise, students should not be satisfied with simple shallow or "yes" or "no" answers. They should be wanting more, thirsty to learn and to absorb knowledge. As teachers, we have the duty of helping students embrace and understand uncertainty and how to deal with it. We must learn how to *empower* these students.

Asking questions is one of the best ways to do this. Questions, according to Taylor (2020), "are at the ground level of what can be done to make our classrooms, either virtual or in person, better." Students should feel safe and empowered to ask as many questions as they have and engage in discussion as much as possible. It is by carrying out this exchange that they will learn, develop, and demonstrate interest in the class. It will also help you, as their educator, to measure what they are learning and what needs to be improved.

By enabling the class to ask questions, you are guiding them toward finding *wisdom*. To understand their values and what is important to them, they develop critical and logical thinking. When you motivate them to speak and to satisfy their curiosity, they might not see it, but you are making them participate and determine how their own learning process is being carried out. This will be the way they will demonstrate their interest and engage in an exchange with you. What can be more gratifying than an engaged class?

Therefore, my approach and my suggestion is to always motivate your students to question. Praise them when they ask questions. If they need to be pushed, you should start the conversation by asking them simple questions, related to the subject, that will demand their participation. Make class a safe environment to ask, where they won't be judged or criticized for doing so. Be the change your students need to be the masters of their own learning. Control the environment in your classroom to ensure this can be done. Separate the time, opportunity, and means to do this.

One of the best ways to approach questioning in class also dates back to the Greek philosophers, just as Stoicism does: the Socratic dialogue. One of the main objectives in using this method is to help you determine if the students were able to understand the content. Let's take a look at how we can implement this method in the classroom.

Socratic dialogue

Even though you might not realize it, you might be engaging your students in the Socratic dialogue during your class. This is because the "modern" method of the ancient teaching technique involves asking a series of simple and open-ended questions that will guide your students to analyze a situation. When you do this, you are engaging your students in class and showing them how they can use critical thinking to solve complex matters. In this case, you must be careful because "the teacher isn't asking questions to see what the student already knows and they should never become a devil's advocate or a debate opponent. Instead, the teacher asks questions to dive deeper into a complex subject" (Hcsuper, 2023).

Although some teachers might find it challenging to implement objective lessons using this method, it is just a matter of adapting the teaching approach. By employing the Socratic dialogue technique, teachers can effectively engage students, maintain control over the classroom, and guide them toward correct reasoning through thought-provoking questions. This interactive exchange between teacher and students encourages reflection and critical thinking. Moreover, it empowers students to express their doubts freely or question concepts they may not comprehend fully.

If this is the case, the teacher should ideally direct their question into another, "forcing" them to think and establish a relationship with the theme that is being taught. You should motivate your students to participate and engage, even if they are somewhat unsure in the beginning how this will work. As you put it in practice more often, they will get better and better at giving you answers and you will see your students thrive—even in other subjects.

When you give students the possibility (and time) to *think* about a solution instead of giving them preestablished answers, you are enabling them to discover the beauty of learning and questioning things. You are giving them the opportunity to participate and engage in a class that before did not interest them. When *you* change *your* approach to teaching and make it a safe place for them to question, discuss, and elaborate a rationale, you will be giving them much more than the ability to "answer questions." You will be teaching them the skills of rational and critical thinking to solve problems, thus helping them practice skills they will be able to use outside school.

Intrinsic value

Students' lack of attention in class stems from the belief that what they learn has no practical application (Goal Valuation, n.d.). This assumption holds due to the rigid educational system and societal neglect of essential elements. Born into a chaotic world, students need more exposure to a broader context and need to grasp the connection between classroom knowledge and real-life relevance. Moreover, our society (and the public school system) can be hypocritical, valuing honesty while stifling free expression and silencing diverse perspectives.

In many public schools, students are denied opportunities to showcase their knowledge and engage in hands-on activities that foster more profound understanding. Budgetary constraints contribute to overcrowded classrooms and demotivated professionals, grappling with limited resources. Apart from financial challenges, there is a resistant attitude toward embracing change and providing students with deserved opportunities for growth.

Most of these things, even though we try, are out of our control. Therefore, we must offer the best educational possibilities with the limited material and resources we are given to work with. And to show value to a student with what we have… well, it is difficult, to say the least. Because of this, teachers must, most of the time, go out of their way to find a way to teach the students in a way that attracts them to the subject and engages them in the lesson. One of the ways to do this is to show them the intrinsic value of what is being taught.

One of the main problems with the modern educational system, according to Burton (2014), is that "[m]any of the students we face are young and not aware that their decisions not to pay attention or see the value in their education can have long lasting effects on their lives." This means they cannot see the use of what they learn in school and how it applies to their lives. They don't understand why history is important, for example, or why it is important to know biology.

To increase involvement and participation in your lesson, you can apply a few tips to ensure they understand its value. They are, according to Vahidi (2015):

- Show how and why the content is important in real life.
- Use additional teaching resources such as games and hands-on experiences.
- Enable your student to ask questions and participate by promoting active learning.
- Challenge them! Some students are motivated by challenges that will defy their knowledge and their rational abilities.
- Give them choices and the option of deciding how they want to learn and the best method to be adopted.
- Provide feedback.
- Apply what is being learned to stories and subjects that might interest them.
- Bring joy, happiness, and enthusiasm to the class.
- Talk *to* them rather than *at* them.

These are a few of my suggestions, but you should feel free to add any other approaches you feel are adequate and can be used to motivate them. If you are in doubt, there is only one way you can be sure it will work: try it out! Based on my experience, at least one of them will have the desired effect and you will see change happen in your classroom (especially with the troublemakers).

The marvelous Stoic educator

As a public school teacher, I often encounter challenging student behavior. One particular student, let's call him Alex, was constantly disruptive and would not listen to my instructions. It was frustrating, and I felt like I was losing control of my classroom.

I remembered the teachings of Stoicism and realized the importance of focusing on what I could control. Even though I couldn't control Alex's disruptive behavior, I knew I could control my reactions. Instead of getting angry or frustrated, I approached Alex with compassion and empathy. I talked to him one-on-one and tried to understand the root cause of his behavior.

Through our conversations, I learned that Alex was dealing with personal issues at home that were affecting his class behavior. I listened to him and showed him that I cared. After that conversation, I devised a plan to secretly help him manage his behavior and handle his personal challenges.

To help Alex stay focused and engaged in class, I gave him specific duties to take care of in the classroom, such as distributing handouts, picking up photocopies for his classmates, erasing the chalkboard, and being the time monitor for class activities. Giving him these responsibilities made him feel a sense of purpose and importance in the classroom.

Applying Stoic principles of compassion and empathy, I was able to turn a challenging situation into a positive one. Alex's behavior improved, and my classroom became a more productive learning environment.

* * *

As a veteran public school teacher with more than two decades of experience, I've developed a pedagogical approach I call "Marvel

Education." This method, which I mentioned earlier in this chapter and will now elaborate on, is built upon genuine care and listening to students, empowering them to overcome challenges and achieve their dreams. Marvel Education incorporates theatrical improvisation, storytelling, Socratic dialogues, introspection, and awe-inspiring moments that encourage students to think outside the box and explore their potential.

Our role as educators transcends the mere dissemination of knowledge. We are entrusted with helping our students discover purpose and relevance in their education. In an era where information is readily accessible through digital tools like ChatGPT, Google, and other apps, what 21st-century students truly yearn for are authentic human connections and experiences. We can achieve greater engagement and a more harmonious classroom dynamic by fostering an environment where students perceive the classroom as a sanctuary for in-person learning and socializing.

When was the last time you had your students in awe of something you were teaching? When did you last employ a fascinating teaching approach that captivated your class? This is the power of giving your students moments that fuel their imagination, creativity, and curiosity. It is the difference between a passive student and one actively engaged with the content.

The rigid methods enforced by the public education system have inadvertently stifled students' curiosity and engagement. Outmoded training and mentoring techniques have dampened the joy of discovery and learning. By embracing innovative approaches and modernizing the educational system, we can rekindle the spark of curiosity and make learning a joyous journey once again. As educators, we hold the power to transform the educational landscape and inspire our students.

What will awe our students? How do we achieve this? Employ various methods to inspire awe in your students. Some may respond to storytelling, others to music, and some to hands-on activities. Each student is unique, and discovering what inspires them requires experimentation. Educators are crucial in helping students find their purpose, sometimes more so than their families.

To determine what works, experiment. Each student will have their own experience, but the goal is to create a method that transcends the classroom and helps students develop a sense of purpose. It's not about what you teach but how you teach it. Just as we feel awe when experiencing art, music, or nature, students want to be inspired and find their place in the world. They seek a sense of awe in their education, which helps maintain their motivation and resilience.

As a Stoic educator, you have the job of guiding students by using the four virtues—wisdom, courage, justice, and temperance—as a roadmap. While you cannot control their circumstances, you can influence how they feel in school, giving them moments of awe. You can help them learn the values and virtues they need to thrive. This journey starts with you, the agent of change. By changing yourself and how you react to the world, you can inspire your students.

Not all students will be awed, and not all will participate actively. When faced with unenchanted students, try to understand them. Accept that you cannot control everything, but focus on what you can influence. This acceptance is crucial for maintaining your own resilience and effectiveness as an educator.

Embracing student voice

I remember the day I faced one of the most challenging classes of my teaching career. These students were disengaged and disrespectful and showed no interest in learning. I felt helpless and frustrated but knew I had to find a way to connect.

While brainstorming ways to manage this challenging class, I came up with an idea for a game I named "Passion Points." I was initially hesitant, unsure if it would work, but I decided to try it. With funny questions, purposely and carefully designed, some dice, and a spinner (that looked like a casino spinner), students were encouraged to share their interests (personal and professional), hobbies, desired knowledge, and so on. By doing this, I obtained information about students' passions and interests.

To my surprise, the game was a success! It engaged even the most disengaged and disruptive students; it allowed me to rethink my lessons and design them around my students' interests. Little by little, they could explore their passions in class (with their classmates) and seemed to have found meaning in their learning. Without knowing, my students started to gain ownership of their education, sharing their interests with each other, and became more enthusiastic and excited to attend class. The most notorious class skippers showed up eagerly for their Spanish class. It was a turning point in the classroom dynamic.

This experience taught me the power of letting students take control of their education. I realized the best way to teach is to let your students lead. The game's success not only inspired me to continue exploring student-centered approaches in my teaching but also filled me with immense joy and satisfaction. The students were so engaged and motivated that day that it encouraged other classmates who had previously skipped class to turn up every day, a testament to the transformative power of student-centered learning.

Witnessing the transformative impact of empowering students to take ownership of their learning journey was a profound revelation. By stepping back and allowing them to lead, I discovered the true essence of effective teaching: creating an environment where students are intrinsically motivated, engaged, and actively shaping their educational experience.

Through this approach, I not only connected with my students on a deeper level but also reignited my passion for teaching. It taught me that a classroom is not just a place for students to learn but a space for them to socialize and connect with real people. This realization has rekindled my passion for teaching and inspired me to create a more engaging and interactive learning environment.

This student-centered approach not only fostered a more meaningful connection with my students but also reignited the very essence of why I chose this noble profession. It reminded me of the importance of creating a nurturing and inclusive learning environment, where students can engage in authentic human interactions and cultivate essential social skills, transcending the virtual barriers of technology. I balanced the use of technology by incorporating it only when it enhanced the learning experience, such as for collaborative projects or accessing additional resources. Technology, when used judiciously, can enhance this process by facilitating collaborative learning and providing access to a wealth of information.

As educators, we have a role that extends beyond imparting knowledge; it involves empowering our students to become active participants in their learning journey. By embracing this philosophy, we can unlock their innate curiosity, creativity, and thirst for knowledge, igniting a lifelong love for learning that will benefit them far beyond the classroom and affirming our integral role in their growth.

The true legacy of a Stoic educator lies in the profound impact we have on our students' lives. By embodying the principles of Stoicism and also fostering a student-centered approach, we not only impart academic knowledge but also cultivate the essential skills and mindsets that enable our students to thrive in an ever-changing world.

Through our unwavering commitment to resilience, mindfulness, and the cultivation of positive relationships, we create a nurturing environment that empowers students to embrace their authentic selves, explore their passions, and develop the confidence to navigate life's challenges with grace and wisdom. Your efforts in fostering this environment are deeply appreciated.

As we approach the culmination of our journey, it becomes clear that the teachings of Stoicism extend far beyond the classroom. In the final chapter, we will explore how the principles of Stoicism, such as resilience in the face of challenges, mindfulness in our interactions, and the cultivation of positive relationships, can be seamlessly integrated into every aspect of our lives, enabling us to live with purpose, integrity, and a deep sense of fulfillment.

Prepare to be inspired and empowered to embrace the Stoic way of life in its entirety. By doing so, we will become not only more effective educators but also more fulfilled human beings, capable of navigating life's challenges with grace, wisdom, and an unwavering commitment to living in accordance with virtue. This personal transformation will not only benefit us but also inspire our students and colleagues.

Bibliography

Burton, M. (2014, February 1). Stoicism & teaching: Part one. *Modern Stoicism*. Retrieved from https://modernstoicism.com/stoicism-teaching-part-one

Goal Valuation. (n.d.). NRC/GT University of Connecticut. Retrieved from https://nrcgt.uconn.edu/underachievement_study/goal-valuation/gv_goalva02

Hcsuper. (2023, January 24). Should educators use the Socratic method of teaching? *Resilient Educator*. Retrieved from https://resilienteducator.com/classroom-resources/should-educators-use-the-socratic-method-of-teaching

Taylor, B. (2020, August 9). Empowerment. *Bptaylor52*. Retrieved from https://bptaylor52.com/2020/08/09/empowerment

Vahidi, S. (2015, June 29). Strategies to increase the intrinsic value of tasks in your class. *The National Research Center on the Gifted and Talented*. Retrieved from https://nrcgt.uconn.edu/underachievement_study/goal-valuation/gv_goalva02

CHAPTER 8

The Stoic Way of Life

Living Virtuously In and Out of the Classroom

DOI: 10.4324/9781003535652-9

❝ It's time you realized that you have something in you more powerful and miraculous than the things that affect you and make you dance like a puppet.

Marcus Aurelius, *Meditations*

Once you start experiencing the difference of adopting a Stoic way of life in the classroom, I am certain you will want to do the same outside the school. At least for me, this was a game-changer in my relationships, the way I started to see adversity in my personal life, and my approach to the way I reacted to adversity when faced with it. There came a moment in which I was able to completely let go of the things I could not control, even though I can confide in you and say that it bothered me—a lot—in the beginning.

I learned to accept that things happen and, sometimes, all that is left to do is accept them. If I had a day out and it started to rain, I thought about alternatives to keep me entertained even though there was a change of plans. I understood better how to interact with friends and family, stopping to accept, think, and breathe before immediately reacting to a feeling. I realized that by considering their point of view, I could find solutions that would better serve everyone and not just myself.

But the change I noticed the most was, incredibly, an increase in my optimism. Although I started practicing negative visualization of all the things that could go wrong during my day, I just couldn't shake off the feeling of acceptance and the peace that it brought me. This does not mean that I no longer reacted and just accepted situations as they were. Not at all. But what I did do was to look adversity in the eye and act according to what I *could* do instead of stressing about the things I *could not* do.

In my opinion, that is the beauty of Stoicism: It enables you to see life with different eyes, from a different point of view, and inevitably become more optimistic about how you live. When you start thinking that this could be your last day, you change and react to things differently. You start pursuing satisfaction, happiness, and fulfillment in everything you do. You learn to make every moment count and ensure that, if this is in fact your last day, you will have lived life to its fullest and be proud of what you were able to accomplish. For this reason, I can affirm that Stoicism changes your life because you start having a positive and optimistic perspective and attitude to life in general.

Stoic optimism

Even after everything I have explained here, some people still associate Stoicism with negativity or lack of emotions. It is OK if you tell someone you are learning about the philosophy and they show little enthusiasm or even reluctance to accept your change. This is the view that people have of Stoicism, not the positive and engaging perspective—they do not see optimism.

Nevertheless, I can affirm, without a shadow of uncertainty, that the Stoic philosophy is positive and, yes, it is optimistic. Where the non-Stoic sees a road block, the Stoic sees opportunity. Where the non-adept acts with emotions that can lead to disastrous consequences, the Stoic works to find a rational and fair reaction to adverse events. Lastly, where non-believers are dwelling on the past, what could be, and the difficulties in life, the Stoic has learned to accept and live the present fully, embracing the positive opportunities.

They accept that some things are just as they should be, and this brings unimaginable freedom. "By accepting the events of my life as simply 'things that happen', and by accepting that it is my interpretation of them that shapes my response, I can begin to embrace what is actually 'up to me'" (Anderson, 2022). When you understand that you are able to control what happens to you, how you feel, and how you will impact the world, this gives us a feeling of empowerment, of being able to deal with any adversity life will throw at us.

You could say that optimism is not exactly what is shown when negative visualization takes place. I differ from this idea. I think that it is exactly by thinking what can go wrong that you will develop solutions to make the issue better. Simply because if there is something you can do about it, it can be remedied. And if it cannot, well, then it is what it is. Honestly, I cannot think about how it would be possible to argue with that. If the store is out of your favorite chocolate, there is nothing you can do about it. You can complain, you can get angry, but you cannot magically make the chocolate appear. On the other hand, you could get rid of the negativity, embrace a positive attitude, and look for the same chocolate in the store in the next block. Who knows, you might find it!

Marcus Aurelius once said, "Our actions may be impeded … but there can be no impeding our intentions or dispositions. Because we can accommodate and adapt. The mind adapts and converts to its own purposes the obstacle to our acting" (Aurelius, 2022). One thing it is essential to learn is that we are the ones responsible for our destinies, and the only thing we are certain of is that we will die one day. Let me ask you something: How much do you worry about other people's opinions? About receiving their approval? About how people will think of you? Why is what they think more important than what you think?

This is not the right way to go. Why are you outsourcing your condition of being happy to others? In addition to this, Gillihan (2020) quotes Marcus Aurelius, who said, "Disturbance comes only from within—from our own perceptions." How much longer are you going to give people the ability to control what you think, feel, or do? No! This is under *your* control. *You control you*—your actions, your feelings, and your thoughts. And, once you learn to accept these, you are going to rationalize and then control, according to *your standards*, the reaction you are going to have according to the situation. It is essential that you understand that it is all a matter of *perception* and the way you see your Stoic self.

Your Stoic self

Suppose you are working on your computer and the lights go out. You have no batteries and cannot continue working. What are you going to do? You are probably going to get upset and frustrated, especially if you were really set on finishing the document today. However, your neighbor was also working on their computer when the lights went out, and they also do not have enough battery. Are you going to get upset because of that? Well, likely not. Possibly because it has nothing to do with you. The same can be said about your neighbor: they will likely be frustrated because they can no longer finish what they were working on, but they could not care less that the same happened to you. In both cases, the situation was important to each of you. Still, it didn't matter as much if it happened to the other person because of your *perceptions*.

When you think about the situation above, what makes you so special that your project was more important than your neighbor's? Why should you be seen as "the special one" and not just another person living in the building that had the lights go off? In the Stoic perception, when we consider this matter objectively, you might understand that "we are no more important than anyone else, and the wise person should learn to see themselves as just one person in the crowd" (Matthias, 2021). If you think about problems from this point of view, you might understand that one individual's problem is *their* own problem and that it is not more important than another person's just because of who they are. We are all the same, just living under different circumstances. Therefore, what is important to me might not be important to you, but it might mean something to someone who is affected by it.

But how do I become this ideal self as envisioned by the Stoics? Well, first and foremost, you must understand that you are not alone in the world; you are just one out of many, and things do not happen with the specific purpose of bothering you. It doesn't start to rain to purposely ruin your day, and the trash truck that is in front of you in traffic going slowly is not doing this just out of spite. It rains because of meteorological conditions, and the truck is going slow because it is doing what it is supposed to do: collect the trash. If you really intend to embrace the Stoic way of life and become your ideal self, I am going to talk about some ways you can do that, which you should put into practice together with everything else you have read in this book.

Stoic practices to help you become your ideal self

If you are thinking about how to start incorporating the best version of yourself, then I could say that you have already started! Just by reading this book, you are gaining knowledge that perhaps you did not have before and you are well on your way to adopting the essential practices of becoming a Stoic. Remember that one of the main virtues of a Stoic is wisdom, and this means not only spreading it but also obtaining it. You can do this through reading, studying, and listening to other people speak. The possibilities are endless as long as you are doing this with a purpose, an objective.

There is no reason to, for example, spend hours scrolling through social media to simply know "what is going on." You must educate yourself through the proper channels that will enable you to obtain knowledge of a subject you want to learn. In addition to this, you must focus on studying things you are going to apply in your life. It is a waste of time to focus on things that have no use in your life. Therefore, you must protect your time and ensure that you are being productive when necessary but that you are also taking the time to rest. To determine the importance of what you are going to do, once again ask yourself: *If this was my last day on earth, did I spend my time learning and doing productive things?* The answer to this question will be enough to tell you if you have been using your time appropriately.

This also means that you should look up to people whom you admire, who could be mentors to you. Epictetus said that we should use people as inspiration: "Invoke the characteristics of the people you admire most and adopt their manners, speech, and behavior as your own" (Holiday, 2020). To do this, use the internet to your advantage. There are several educational and informative videos with interviews, courses, and teaching from great people who live during our time and some who were here before us. These people should inspire you to be like them, act like them, and, especially, think like them when adversity knocks on your door. Think how this individual would solve the matter and how they would react.

You should always keep in mind that following your values and beliefs is the key to living a fulfilling life. Incorporate and practice the Stoic mindset into your life. First thing in the morning, think about what you want to accomplish and how you are going to do that. Decide that you will not allow anyone to make you lose your patience and that you will not act impulsively based on your feelings. Reflect and rationalize before doing so.

Start with simple actions that can go a long way. Express gratitude. Give forgiveness. Improve daily. Convey wisdom. Love. Be kind to others. Face your fears. Act with consciousness. If you feel like there is a situation in which there is injustice, have the courage to face it, intervene, and make it right. If you do not feel you can add anything positive to the matter, refrain from engaging, accept it as it is. Choose to be calm and undisturbed rather than putting yourself in challenging and adverse situations. Take things step by step as you learn and gain knowledge and experience.

Practice self-control, always observing yourself. Refrain from engaging in excess or in passiveness. Live your life with the temperance of a person who knows that they are not owed anything and that everyone has the same rights. If there is conflict, ensure that you are looking at the situation from all angles. Remember that conflict is not necessarily bad; it could be an opportunity to obtain justice. You should not look for the easy way out; embracing the challenges life gives you will make you better at dealing with those that are about to come.

Life will always have obstacles, adversities, and negative situations. Their outcome and how they affect your life will depend on you and only on you. *You are the one who can control how these situations affect you.* Whether they are external or internal, it will be up to you to manage these feelings that will arise and not react to them. The world is not out there to attack you—things are simply the way they are. It will be up to you to be distressed by these events or not. However, remember that if nothing can be done, then it can't be changed, and if nothing can be changed, all that is left to do is accept it. Learn to expect the unexpected and deal with uncertainty. To hope for the best but plan for the worst—isn't that how the popular saying goes?

Lastly, keep in mind that toxic people are everywhere, there is no running away from them, so you must learn how to deal with them. How you do this will give you a greater, or lesser, calm and perspective of life. Everyone has their own issues, their own lives, experiences, and backgrounds. Each of us lives and has a different perspective on life. Don't assume that you know what is going on unless you are told. Even then, if you have nothing productive, encouraging, or positive to say, it is best to remain silent.

Adopting the Stoic lifestyle might be a significant change to what you are used to. It might (and likely will) greatly impact your lifestyle. It could include finding a different meaning to everything you believe. It will be difficult at first. It will be demanding, I won't lie. But the results will show—trust me, you will see life change right before your eyes. A change for the better, guided toward happiness and completion. Toward fulfillment in your life in and out of school. It will improve your personal and work relationships. You will learn how to see life from an optimistic point of view and, most importantly, you will feel free. Free to control and guide your life as you see fit.

Adopting a Stoic lifestyle

A s a teacher who tries to embody Stoic principles, I strive to maintain a sense of calm and resilience in my teaching practice and daily life. The best way to teach is to empower students to take control of their education and find meaning in their lives.

One experience that comes to mind was attending a post-observation meeting with my principal. The principal was waiting for me in his office, where he opened his laptop and began giving me feedback from his computer without looking at me. He seemed more concerned with completing a checklist than genuinely conversing about my teaching practice and the specific lesson he observed. His comments were general and vague; although they sounded positive, they had nothing to do with me or the class he had observed days before. When I asked him specific (outside-the-box) questions that demanded deep thinking, it was apparent he could not organically carry on. He was so lost in the systematic method of doing things that he could not even listen to what I was asking or think critically. I felt like I was being evaluated by a machine rather than a human being.

It was unfortunate to see. It leads me to think of the current state of our obsolete educational system, full of automaton individuals who are not interested in education; they are in those positions just for the money. Despite this, I remained calm and focused on what I could control. I listened carefully to the principal's feedback but knew that the recommendations were not organic but based on a rubric and form prepared by the Department of Education. I was determined to improve my teaching practice not to satisfy a template but to truly help my students; they are why I became a teacher.

****

Daily, I try to embody Stoic principles by focusing on what I can control and not letting external circumstances affect my inner peace. I advocate for my colleagues by standing up for what's right and offering support when needed. Embodying Stoic principles in our teaching practice and daily life can create a positive and inspiring classroom environment for our students while being a voice for change in the education system.

It is not always easy to embody Stoic principles in the face of challenges, but by doing so, we can become better educators and individuals. What to do with a toxic system? There is nothing we can do; keep working to fulfill our mission, remembering that our mission as teachers is to pass on the light of knowledge—this is something we can control.

Bibliography

Anderson, P. (2022, May 2). Stoics are optimists. *LinkedIn*. Retrieved from https://www.linkedin.com/pulse/stoics-optimists-peter-anderson-phd-acc-cec/?trk=pulse-article_more-articles_related-content-card\

Aurelius, M. (2022). *Meditations*. East India Publishing Company.

Gillihan, S. (2020, September 24). How to stop outsourcing your happiness. *Conscious Connection*. Retrieved from https://www.consciousconnection magazine.com/2020/09/how-to-stop-outsourcing-your-happiness/

Holiday, R. (2020, January 2). 7 Stoic practices to help you become your ideal self in 2020. *Daily Stoic*. Retrieved from https://dailystoic.com/7-stoic-practices-to-help-you-become-your-ideal-self-in-2020/

Matthias, A. (2021, December 13). The Stoic view of the self. *Daily Philosophy*. Retrieved from https://daily-philosophy.com/the-stoic-view-of-the-self/

Conclusion

A New Chapter Begins

DOI: 10.4324/9781003535652-10

Congratulations! You now have all the tools and essential knowledge to become a Stoic educator! I am thrilled that you have joined me on this path, and I hope that our exploration has provided you with valuable insights and practical tools to navigate the challenges of the educational system. Together, we have uncovered alternatives to stress, burnout, and disappointment, empowering you to reshape your perspective and find fulfillment in your role as an educator. I am glad you were able to take this journey with me, and I hope that I have been able to help you see some alternative ways to navigate the challenging school environment we have to deal with. According to my experience, if you use the tools and methods I have shared with you, such as practicing negative visualization and applying the dichotomy of control, you will be able to change how you see your day as a teacher.

Throughout this book, my primary objective was to show you that there are alternatives to being stressed, burned out, and nervous and feeling the disappointment often experienced in the public school system. You must understand the most crucial point to determine your journey as a Stoic educator: let go of the things you cannot control. By releasing our attachment to external factors, we create space for inner peace and regain a sense of empowerment. Let it go if you cannot take positive action or add value to something. There is no fault in doing this, just as you should feel no guilt in deciding not to take action.

In the realm of control, exercising mastery over our thoughts, actions, and feelings is paramount. When faced with authoritarian principals, unresponsive secretaries, complaining colleagues, or challenging students, pausing, reflecting, and breathing become crucial. We can effectively manage these situations by considering fairness, wisdom, and alignment with desired outcomes in our responses. This intentional shift in mindset, accompanied by stopping, thinking, and taking a breath, empowers us to navigate challenging circumstances. It bridges the gap between accepting our emotions and taking appropriate action, making all the difference in our approach. For instance, when dealing with unresponsive administrators, document your concerns and seek support from your colleagues or professional organizations.

In any situation, it is vital to recognize the potential for control and its impact on the outcome. Whether it involves resolving conflicts, managing the classroom, or navigating bureaucratic obstacles, your actions are pivotal in shaping results. Maintaining the status quo will likely lead to stagnant circumstances and continued dissatisfaction. However, you can bring about remarkable shifts by proactively modifying your behavior and approach, even within the classroom setting. Embracing this opportunity to influence situations positively can lead to transformative changes and a more fulfilling professional experience. Seize the chance to create a positive outcome, knowing that your actions are vital to unlocking new possibilities.

As you embrace Stoicism as an educator and incorporate mindfulness into your teaching practice, you will witness remarkable transformations in your students. They will not only become more engaged and focused but also start appreciating the value of education. By guiding them and demonstrating that learning can be enjoyable, you will help them develop critical thinking skills and foster a sense of awe in the school environment. This is the power of mindfulness: it allows you to observe this positive change firsthand, empowering you to impact your students' educational journey profoundly. Embrace these principles, adopt mindfulness, and witness the incredible transformation that unfolds.

In the face of toxic coworkers, disorderly students, and a rigid bureaucratic system, it is crucial not to let these challenges dampen your motivation and passion for your chosen profession. Refuse to allow negative influences to overshadow the joy of teaching. Instead, change your perspective, alter your view of these obstacles, and take action where you can make a difference. Remember, always to do your best, as your students deserve nothing less. By staying resilient and maintaining a positive mindset, you can overcome these challenges and continue to inspire and nurture the young minds that depend on you. Let your dedication and unwavering commitment shine through as you create a positive and impactful educational experience for your students.

Several years ago, while teaching at a public school in New York City, I faced a challenging student whom I will refer to as Laura. Laura's behavior disrupted my lessons, as she would frequently scream, curse, and hurl insults at me in Spanish. Drawing on my admiration for Stoic practices, I strived to remain calm, composed, and respectful. Despite my attempts not to engage directly with Laura, her constant demand for attention escalated. Frequently, I had to ask her to leave the classroom, a measure that the school administration discouraged. While I preferred not to resort to such measures, protecting the learning environment for the 33 other students in the class was necessary. When a student hinders others' learning, I firmly believe they must be removed from the classroom. I exhausted all options, attempting different approaches and seeking assistance from the administration when necessary. However, in that school, the administration's response varied, ranging from cooperation to blame-shifting, which can be comically unfair.

In public schools, teachers are often held 100% responsible for their students' behavior, which is unjust. Disruptive incidents with Laura persisted despite my best efforts, and the administration offered no meaningful assistance. Furthermore, the administration resented me because of my complaints about various irregularities within the school. For instance, one assistant principal deliberately scheduled one-on-one meetings during my lunch period, which was dedicated to my religious activities, despite my explicit request—at the beginning of the school year—to avoid such conflicts. Reporting these incidents to the Office of Human Rights led to a change in his practice. However, it is possible that, in retaliation, the administration failed to provide any support in dealing with Laura (they wouldn't support other teachers either).

It came down to contacting Laura's mother for the fourth time. The phone conversation in which I addressed her daughter's misbehavior in class was conducted entirely in Spanish because of her limited English proficiency. I used a Spanish idiom or simile to convey the magnitude of the student's verbal disrespect toward me. In Spanish, I said to the mother, "*Señora, cada vez que esa niña abre la boca parece una letrina*" ("Ma'am, every time that girl opens her mouth it looks like a latrine"). Here, I just gave you a literal translation in English, but since it was a fixed phrase in Spanish, the literal translation to English is NOT accurate. In Spanish, the phrase I used captures the notion of a "dirty mouth." However, given the nature of Spanish as a Romance language, it incorporates numerous fixed phrases that do not have a direct translation in English, as their literal interpretation would fail to convey the intended meaning effectively.

It is essential to understand the relationship between language and thought, as languages are not merely tools of communication but also frameworks for thinking and perceiving the world. To illustrate this, let us consider the difference between fixed phrases in Spanish and English. For instance, when someone says "Thank you" in English, the typical response is "You're welcome." However, in Spanish, this is translated as "De nada." While "De nada" is often translated as "You're welcome," the phrase carries a more profound cultural significance. It is associated with the Roman Catholic notion that a good religious person must continually perform unlimited acts of kindness for others, remaining humble and refraining from boasting about their deeds. The belief is that one should never cease doing good, as God will compensate them in the Afterlife or Paradise. Thus, the expression "De nada" embodies this concept of limitless giving; that's why the specific deed someone performs is considered "nothing."

On the other hand, the English phrase "You're welcome" serves as an acknowledgment, implicitly conveying that the speaker has done something good for the person expressing gratitude. This fundamental difference in meaning highlights the existence of various fixed phrases across languages. By recognizing fixed phrases' cultural and linguistic nuances, we gain a deeper understanding of language as a vessel for thought and perception. It reminds us that literal translations may not always capture an expression's essence and intended meaning. These examples provide a glimpse into the complexity of languages and the significance of fixed phrases in conveying ideas and cultural values.

As a result of that conversation with Laura's mother in which I used that fixed phrase, I was reported, and the school administration accused me of corporal punishment despite my weeks of reporting incidents involving Laura. In the subsequent meetings, I attempted to explain the context and linguistic nuances. Still, the administration was unwilling to listen and proceeded with "an investigation." I suggested they consult a linguist to ensure the accuracy of their investigation since it involved fixed phrases in Spanish. However, the case was eventually dropped without any further communication from the administration.

Interestingly, owing to numerous irregularities, the city later closed the school where these incidents occurred. As for Laura, she stopped attending my class, although I heard reports from fellow teachers that her cursing and disruptive behavior persisted in others. This anecdote illustrates how I have approached these difficulties in the New York City Department of Education with a Stoic mindset, maintaining resilience in the face of challenges and striving for fairness and effective classroom management.

As we conclude, my ultimate wish is for you to discover, in this book, an alternative method to navigate the daily challenges you face as an educator. It all starts with taking that first step and progressing from there. Embrace practices like negative visualization, conflict management, and problem-solving. As you engage in these endeavors, the journey becomes increasingly effortless. Remember, you already possess the inherent capability to become a Stoic educator with the tools and wisdom to bring about positive transformation. It is time to put your knowledge into action and make a difference. Believe in yourself and embrace the possibilities that lie ahead. You have the power to accomplish this!

I invite you to embrace this journey fully and witness its profound impact on your life and the lives of your students. Your commitment to creating a nurturing and empowering learning environment is essential. Let the principles of Stoicism guide you as you forge a new path that exemplifies resilience, wisdom, and compassion.

As we conclude our journey, remember that your influence extends far beyond the confines of the classroom. You are shaping the future by shaping young minds. Believe in your abilities, trust the process, and know you are making a difference. With the power of Stoicism as your guiding light, a new chapter begins—one filled with growth, fulfillment, and endless possibilities.

Printed in the United States
by Baker & Taylor Publisher Services